My Mother's House

My Mother's House

a memoir

DAVID ARMAND

Texas Review Press
Huntsville, Texas

FIRST EDITION

Author's Photo by Lucy Armand
Cover Photo by Edward M. Alba, Sr.

The characters, incidents, and dialogue are drawn from the author's memory and perceptions of his life events. They are not intended to be defamatory toward any person, living or dead. In all instances, the author has stayed truthful to his experiences.

Requests for permissions to reproduce material from this work should be sent to: Texas Review Press, English Department, Sam Houston State University, P.O. Box 2146, Huntsville, TX 77341-2146

The author would like to express his sincere gratitude to Paul Ruffin, Kimberly Davis, Elizabeth Evans, and Catherine Smith of Texas Review Press for their editorial guidance and suggestions. Thanks also to Dixon Hearne and Kevin Cutrer for reading early drafts and offering sensitive feedback; and to Denton Loving and Darnell Arnoult for publishing an extended excerpt from this memoir, titled "Real Work," in *Drafthorse: A Literary Journal of Work and No Work*.

Library of Congress Cataloging-in-Publication Data

Armand, David, 1980- author.
My mother's house / David Armand.
Huntsville, Texas : Texas Review Press, [2016]
LCCN 2015047093 (print) | LCCN 2015047467 (ebook) | ISBN 9781680030730 (pbk. : alk. paper) | ISBN 9781680030747 (e-book)
Armand, David, 1980- | Armand, David, 1980—Childhood and youth. | Armand, David, 1980—Homes and haunts—Louisiana. | Novelists, American—21st century—Biography. | Children of schizophrenics—Louisiana—Biography. | Novelists, American—21st century—Family relationships. | Mothers and sons—Louisiana. | Louisiana—Social life and customs.
Classification: LCC PS3601.R55 Z46 2016 (print) | LCC PS3601.R55 (ebook) | DDC 813/.6—dc23
LC record available at http://lccn.loc.gov/2015047093

This book is dedicated to my mother,
who I think will still love me if she reads it.

My Mother's House

Prologue

My mother smells of urine, feces, the body odor that comes from the over-production of the chemical trans-3-methyl-2-hexenoic acid, and rotten food. This is the smell of schizophrenia. Her house smells equally bad, if not worse. She lives on several small conjoined lots that are all overgrown with weeds and trees. What little of the yard is cleared is littered with old, rusted appliances, insulation that has been torn from under one of her trailers by raccoons; there are feral dogs and cats, rats, and hordes of garbage.

When Hurricane Katrina brought in a nearly thirty-foot storm surge from the Gulf of Mexico, it flooded her trailer, coming up past the roof, from which she and her husband had to swim to a nearby pine tree and hang on until the storm finally passed and the surge receded. To this day, nearly ten years after the storm, she still has the two mobile homes that were flooded out sitting on her property—they are uninhabitable, yet she spends a fair amount of her time in them and refuses (even when FEMA offered to remove them for free, and then even after they demanded the trailers be removed since they were considered a health hazard) to get rid of them. There are blankets of black mold growing up the torn walls and drooping ceilings. Both of the trailers are without electricity, but have dangerous lengths of extension cord running along the warped floors, little electric light bulbs hanging from various exposed rafters. She keeps a sleeping bag on the floor next to piles of damp and moldy clothes, old books, waterlogged papers, and scores of bottles of shampoo, toothpaste, herbal supplements and vitamins, cassette tapes, VHS tapes, old TV Guides (even though she doesn't have or watch a TV), crumpled sheet music, boxes, folders, random manuals, water bottles filled with urine and/or brown water, rolls of toilet paper, large paint buckets which she uses to go to the bathroom.

Along the walls are hundreds of water-stained index cards with notes written on them in her now-choppy, all capital letter handwriting (her penmanship changes from a nice cursive when she's somewhat lucid and calm to an almost angry scrawl when she's frustrated or upset). On the cards are notes from her now-deceased husband warning her (and the world, presumably) about the poison that's in food, how hamburgers cause cancer, the locations of government satellites that were used to create Hurricane Katrina in the Gulf of Mexico, thus starting America's attempt to move its citizens away from the coastlines of our country so that the Chinese will have room to set up their nuclear arsenals. There are lists with days and years when certain, random, unknown people died and their causes of death. Phone numbers, addresses, dates. The times and dates when particular bodily functions were accomplished.

One of the trailers is actually an old camper in which my mother used to live with her husband until the hurricane, a good two decades. That camper is still there, too, in even worse condition than the trailer. It is probably less than two hundred square feet, almost completely filled with garbage, mainly empty cases of Busch beer and their scattered crushed cans, old moldy books and sheet music, more gardening manuals, those ubiquitous *herbal supplements and vitamin bottles, most of them empty or half-filled with rusty brown water and a skein of mosquito eggs. Just outside in the thick growth are more extension cords, none of them functional, old tools covered by a sheet of rusted tin, dirty bedsheets, an old rusted-out pickup truck whose tires have rotted into the ground, and about twenty, five-gallon plastic gas tanks in its bed.*

There are pairs of dirty and torn men's underwear hanging from some of the spindly tree branches, broken plates, old glasses, ashtrays, and pieces of cracked, damp plywood forming a sort of walkway over the muddy, uneven ground. There are broken ladders, wheelbarrows, dog cages, piles of gravel, old stoves and refrigerators, their compressors either torn out by thieves or simply left rusting beside the dead appliances. There are flashlights, batteries, soggy maps, pairs of jeans that have been half-buried in the ground, a shoe here or there, a split garden hose that my mother showers under.

My mother keeps an old camping tent on the dilapidated back porch of the other trailer, the one where she spends most of her time. Inside the tent is an old sleeping bag, some water bottles half-filled with that brown water (which she drinks), and a couple of empty bottles of Vitamin B and Melatonin. She says when it gets too hot outside (and often in South Mississippi the temperature can climb into the upper nineties with one hundred percent humidity and a heat index of one-hundred and fourteen degrees) she sleeps in the tent on the back porch. From there you can hear the large rats skittering around inside the trailer, which she says often wake her up in the middle of the night as they scamper across her legs or her chest. She never seems perturbed by this, simply laughs about it. The thought of a rat the size of a small Chihuahua makes me cringe.

But all of this makes sense to my mother: she's a hoarder, in addition to her myriad other afflictions, and each one of these items that I see as garbage or as having been ruined by the hurricane, holds a special memory to her, all have some potential future use, if serving no other purpose than to become mine when she dies. I've fantasized about pouring gasoline over all of this and just watching it burn.

My mother dresses in men's clothes: oversized hiking shoes from Goodwill, a pair of jeans that used to belong to me, old T-shirts with sweat stains under the arms and grease stains from her hair at the shoulders and in the back. Dandruff and flakes of dead skin are sprinkled over her clothes like salt. To exacerbate the odor of her illness, my mother never takes baths or brushes her teeth. Her teeth are orange and you can see the white plaque around her red-rimmed and irritated gums. Some of her teeth are black and chipped (once, while I was talking to her, one of her teeth actually broke off and fell out of her mouth. She later kept the piece of chipped, black tooth and put it in her pocket for God knows what purpose). Her hair is long and unkempt: it is gray and thick and wiry like the mane of a horse and she never brushes it. She holds it back from her often-scabbed face with an old rubber band. She picks at her skin when she's nervous or upset, which is most of the time. She doesn't shave, so she has a lip of straggly white hair, more sporadic hairs sprouting from her chin like a goat, and if she holds her arm out a particular way, you can see the black nest of hair under her arms through her shirtsleeve. Her legs, which she's fond of pulling up her jeans to scratch on occasion, are equally as hairy and are covered with dried, dead skin and dark lesions. She's physically hard to be around. When I've taken her with me anywhere in public, people stare at her and try to keep their distance.

Her eyes are wide and wild, darting around from side to side like a frightened animal. When she talks to you, she likes to get very close to your face and lock her eyes onto you as though she's holding you into some intense focus. But she also has a nearly impeccable memory—names, dates, conversations: she can remember it all in startling detail. She is a human almanac. She can still sit in front of a piano, even after not playing one for over ten years, and play

"Clair de Lune" from memory, no sheet music, just those beautiful notes playing in her otherwise chaotic mind. It's the only thing, other than drawing, that calms her.

My biggest fear as an adolescent was that I would grow up to be just like my mother. I would wait for the signs to kick in: hearing voices, becoming paranoid, disorganized, confused, angry. I'm thirty-five years old now and none of those things has happened to me, so I feel I can safely say that I'm in the clear. I have learned to counter and to control any possible inclination I might have toward schizophrenia. Instead, I suffer from obsessive-compulsive disorder—the need to check things again and again, to maintain a rigid order and structure in every aspect of my life. My mother suffers from this as well, but it manifests itself in a different form: she'll often repeat herself or have the person who may be speaking to her repeat him or herself so that she can be sure she heard it. She may flick a light switch on and off a dozen times or rub her fingers over a doorknob for several minutes before she's certain it's locked. I've been known to do that myself. Thankfully, that's all my mother gave me of herself, save for maybe her crooked smile and blue eyes.

I love my mother and yet I hate who she is, the disease that has ravaged her mind and her body and her life, which had started to eat away at my life, too, like a cancer, before I had to finally sever ties with her altogether. That's not to say we're not connected in some strange way that mothers and their children are innately bound. We are. It's just that I could never tell her that. Because while I truly believe that she would understand it and even recognize that connection herself, the disease has already killed her, and now she is just living out her life and waiting for it to finally be over with.

Part One

1980s

1.

My first memory is of a white door. I can remember almost every detail of it: the saucer of hardened fingertip skin just above the knob, the red-white-and-blue NASA emblem painted on the front. Both of these details are attributable to my uncle, who told me later in my life that he was the one who painted the NASA emblem and that it was his skin entombed there just beneath it. He told me that he was playing with a tube of super glue when he was a kid and that he had glued his finger to the inside of the door. Since it was late at night, he didn't want to wake his parents (my grandparents) so he took a straight razor that he used for making model cars and sliced the tip of his finger off; nothing gruesome, understand, just the calloused part of skin at the end of his thumb. When his hand was free, he painted over the hard, glued flesh to cover up the evidence. Later, when that room became mine, I would stand behind the white door and rub my small fingers over the tiny saucer, wondering what that strange shape was.

I was standing behind this white door and holding it closed against the screaming and fighting that was taking place on the other side. My mother was screaming at my grandmother, and my uncle was there. I don't know if he was screaming too, but he was likely trying to break up the fight. He would've been in his twenties then, I think, and he still lived at home, along with my mother (who was a single mom), me, and my grandparents. I was probably about two years old when all of this was happening. It was just before I was taken away from my mother for good.

When I heard the fighting move toward the front of the house, I slowly opened the white door and stepped out into the hallway. I crept up the stairs to the kitchen and followed the yelling to the living room. I could see my grandmother standing at the front door of the house. She was standing there and peering outside and so I ran toward her and hid behind her leg, holding on to her pants. I was crying.

Then I looked from around my grandmother's leg and out of the opened door toward the driveway. I could see my mother getting inside of her large car and backing it onto the mangled street. She was driving very fast. Too fast for the street we lived on. Like many other streets in New Orleans, it was in deplorable condition: roots from the myriad oak trees grew underneath it, raising the concrete into large dark mounds. The roadway was cracked and there were huge potholes in places, big enough to destroy your car if you weren't careful and didn't drive very slowly. My mother didn't seem to notice these, though (or she simply didn't care) because as soon as she had her car on the road, she began to speed off toward Paris Avenue.

I've played this next image in my head so many times over the years that it starts to seem unreal, like a dream I had a long time ago, like something that didn't even really happen, but I know that it did: my mother speeding toward Paris Avenue, me crying from behind my grandmother's leg for my mommy not to leave, then my uncle leaping onto the hood of my mother's speeding car, trying to get her to stop. Instead of stopping, though, my mother swerved her car from one side of the road to the other in an effort to throw her younger brother off the hood and into the street. I don't know how, but somehow he held on.

My grandmother picked me up and put me in the passenger seat of her baby blue Pontiac Bonneville and then she quickly backed out of the driveway as well. The shade of the large banana trees along the edge of the driveway covered us intermittently as the large leaves brushed up against the windshield and I could hear the rear of the car scrape against the street as we went over the curb and onto the road.

My grandmother was talking to herself as she drove, cursing and chain-smoking Carlton cigarettes as she sped down Paris Avenue after my mother's swerving car. I was curled up on the floorboard now and still sobbing so I couldn't see my mother's car in front of us on the road or what it was doing, but I could picture her in my two-year-old mind speeding down the four-lane street, swerving over potholes and trying to get her brother off the hood of her car. About five minutes later, we pulled into the parking lot of an Exxon station at the corner of Paris Avenue and Robert E. Lee Boulevard. My uncle was standing next to one of the islands of gas pumps, but my mother was gone. We didn't know where she had taken off to, and it was a good two weeks before she came back home. When she finally did, I was taken from her custody.

2.

I was born David Brian Alba on January 20, 1980, to my mother, Susan Elizabeth Alba, who was herself just twenty-nine years old. My mother was not married when she had me and had been encouraged to abort the pregnancy, but because of her stubborn nature (or simply because she didn't want to terminate the life that was growing inside of her, despite her knowing how hard the world was likely going to be on that growing life) she decided to have me anyway. Her subsequent pregnancies, I would later learn (and there were several), would be aborted.

My mother lived with her parents and her younger brother as she tried to raise me in a house that was often in turmoil. My grandmother was an alcoholic, my grandfather a stoic (though loving) businessman who was rarely home. After my mother first had me, things started off pretty well. She was functioning normally, even doted over me, reading to me at night and playing whatever games I wanted to play. But eventually the mornings came when she refused to get out of bed, leaving me to lie beside her in the dark with a full diaper and nothing to eat. Like her, I was often left un-bathed, in need of sunlight, fresh air, attention. Ultimately, when the pressure of being a single mother living in her parents' house got to be too much, my mother would disappear. She would be gone for days or weeks at a time, leaving me to the care of my grandmother, who was also doting and over-protective, but sometimes to a fault.

During these times when my mother was gone, she would go to bars, meet with men, use drugs, and generally try to escape the lot that had become her life. It wasn't having me that made her act like this, though. I was just another card stacked against her favor. My mother was actually behaving this way before I was even born. Promiscuous, abusing drugs and alcohol, acting recklessly. (She once told me that I was conceived because my biological father had some Quaaludes that he wanted to give her in exchange for sex. This "father" would never claim me as his son, and my birth certificate has the word UNKNOWN typed under the FATHER heading. This always seemed an ominous start to my life.)

My mother continued to party and use drugs throughout her pregnancy with me: Xanax, cocaine, alcohol, other prescription medications that she used to numb herself. Once I was born, I was by some miracle in good physical health, at least on the surface. But when I was about a year and a half old, my mother was changing my diaper and found it full of blood. She took me to the hospital, where after some tests, the doctors discovered a tumor on one of my kidneys.

I was given my last rites and was sent to surgery. The doctors were able to remove the afflicted organ, and I was scheduled a rigorous dose of chemotherapy, which was injected into my skin intravenously. On one of these occasions, the nurse or doctor who was administering the drug "spilled" some of it onto my foot, causing a great orbicular burn on my right foot. The next time, oddly enough, some of the chemical was spilled in almost the exact same spot on my left foot, causing a symmetrical scar that was so perfectly similar to the other one, I grew up thinking that everyone had those circular marks on their feet.

Although I survived the cancer, the subsequent hospital visits, the time in intensive care, and the rounds of chemotherapy, my physical state was constantly hampered by being perpetually kept indoors. I was always pale (probably due to a Vitamin D deficiency) and I was always sick with a cold. I had dark circles under my eyes, tiny pink rashes on my legs.

To make my physical appearance even more grotesque, I had a dark gray tooth in the front of my mouth from when I had fallen down the staircase that led from the kitchen into the hallway where my bedroom was. On top of that, I had a lazy eye that two surgeries were unable to straighten out, so I had to wear a white patch taped over my eye. The patch was actually taped more across my face, covering the top half of my cheek and the side of my nose and even some of my forehead. It was alternated from side to side each week, but my weak eye muscles never straightened out. To this day, you can still see my eye turning inward, as though I'm looking at something behind you.

I was an odd child. Not just physically, but since I spent my first couple of years in a house that was full of adults, I grew up mimicking adult behavior: I enjoyed sitting at the kitchen table and listening to the grown-ups talk, watching them drink and smoke. I probably did this more than I actually played with toys. The adults in my family, noticing this, encouraged me to act older than my actual age, buying me books to read, encouraging my intellectual development at a young age. When most children were playing in the dirt and with dolls, I was playing with an electronic Pac Man video game that my mother had gotten for me at the dime store. The cashier told her I was much too young for the toy, that it was made for children at least twice my age, but my mother bought it for me anyway and I quickly mastered it. Eventually, I got bored with it, though, and took it apart to see how it worked. I was kind of disappointed to see that it was really just composed of a series of small, variegated lights that lit up behind a perforated sheet of black plastic paper, creating the illusion that Pac Man was moving through a maze, chasing after and being chased by ghosts.

My mother also kept a scrap book for me those first couple of years of my life. In it are slips of paper and receipts with her then-neat cursive outlining my achievements and some of the outlandish things she claims I did or said: when I was just six months old, she claims I was speaking in complete sentences, expressing how I felt physically and how I would want her to change my environment: "Could you turn off the light, it's bothering my eyes," she recorded on a sheet of yellow tablet paper, claiming I told her that one evening before bed. The scrap book also contained locks of my white-blonde hair, cards from relatives, immunization records, a picture from the day I was born, and the seemingly endless stack of notepaper listing my favorite foods, favorite sayings, and my favorite songs (I used to have a little 45RPM record player on which I would play Hall 'n' Oates's "Maneater," Kenny Rogers's "The Gambler," and Queen's "Another One Bites the Dust" incessantly. The "Maneater" record was a transparent red color and I liked to hold it up to the light and look through the limned vinyl, casting my whole room the color of blood).

One evening my grandfather took my mother and me out to a business dinner at an upscale restaurant in New Orleans. He would often take my mother with him on occasions such as these since my grandmother often didn't want to go herself. (Or they both had simply decided that it would be better for everyone if my grandmother and mother were separated. All during the day while my grandfather was at work, my mother and grandmother fought. Knives were pulled. The police were called. If my grandfather was ever called home from the office to deal with this, he would say in his angered, tight-lipped fashion that he had a lawyer who would take care of it. Then the police would leave, but not before pointing out how badly my grandmother smelled of whiskey—and it was only one in the afternoon, they'd say. They'd drive away and my grandfather would go back to work, where he could escape, and then my mother and grandmother would go back in the house with me in tow. If things got really bad, it wasn't unheard of for my grandmother to lock my mother in her bedroom, my mother pounding on the door and screaming for hours on end to be let out, me in the other room trying not to hear her, and my grandmother sitting at the kitchen table or leaning against the counter next to my wooden high chair and the pea green rotary phone on the wall where she could see out the bay window onto the driveway, the whole while smoking one after another from her box of Carlton cigarettes and sipping her Evan Williams with water, chasing it with room temperature Budweiser from a can.)

So it was a welcomed reprieve, I'm sure, when my grandfather took both my young mother and me to his business dinner that night. It would give my grandmother a break from us. The dinner consisted of architects and their wives, other engineers, contractors, and politicians who controlled who got

19

what contracts for what jobs. It was an important meeting.

At some point during the meal, after being quiet and attentive to the adult conversations as I often was, I looked up from the table at everyone, as if about to give a toast, and announced loudly, surely at a volume by which most of the restaurant's patrons could hear me, "Fuck it!"

You could hear forks clinking down on plates, napkins ruffling in the silence that hung in the atmosphere now. No one said anything, so I said it again: "Fuck it!"

My grandfather looked over at me, then at my mother, as if to tell her to take me away from the table, to do something. But instead she started laughing. I looked over at her, and thinking I had done something worth her amusement, I started to repeat myself over and over: Fuck it fuck it fuck it fuck it. The whole while my mother was becoming more and more hysterical with laughter as my grandfather finally stood up and told her to take me outside. That was enough, he said.

My mother was like a child herself, reveling in the moment of her two-year-old son repeating one of her very own oft-used phrases like a parrot just learning to squawk out a new word— she laughed and laughed, not wanting to leave.

"Awe, come on, Dad, it's cute," she said.

"Susie," my grandfather said through pinched lips, "take him outside now."

My mother could sense his rage, knew how it tended to boil inside of him, simmer sometimes for hours before he would finally stand up from the kitchen table at night and start throwing dishes across the room, the food and glass hitting the wall and then sliding down to the floor in a steaming heap. How he had kicked holes in the doors, punched the walls. This was the look he wore now.

So my mother took me outside and waited while my grandfather paid the bill, then put us in the car, slamming his door and speeding the whole way back home, never saying a word to either one of us.

3.

I was taken in by my mother's younger sister and her husband shortly after the "car" incident, my first memory. They already had two kids of their own, were only in their early twenties themselves, and were just starting out as adults. My adoptive father made decent money as an electrician then and they had a small brick house in New Orleans East, a nice car, a boat. My adoptive father, Bryan (whom I shortly started to call "Dad"), was the one mainly responsible for taking me in, as he had a hard time watching how I was being raised by my biological mother and her parents. He would sit with my mother for hours, convincing her that giving me up was the right thing to do, that it was the best decision for everyone. Eventually, she agreed, and I moved in with him and my Aunt Gretchen (whom I started to call "Mom" not long after).

Moving into a new environment with new rules, a different structure, and two other kids was difficult, not to mention the trauma of being separated from my biological mother (whom I started to refer to as "Susie" by this point). I was an abnormally cautious, often terrified, little boy. I refused to go outside, I was petrified of dogs, and I didn't play well with my new siblings. I was used to being the center of attention, not having to share my time or my needs with others.

I refused to use the bathroom, only content to hide behind a bedroom door and relieve myself in my own pants. I had violent outbursts and tantrums, attacking my younger brother, hurting animals, hurting myself. I was apparently so disturbed that my new mom took me to a child psychologist shortly after taking me into her home.

But the home in which I was living was not an Edenic one. My dad was a budding alcoholic himself, he was young, and he had a personality that caused him to always feel compelled to prove himself to everyone around him. One afternoon, my new sister and brother and I were playing in the den when someone knocked on the front door. My mom came out from the kitchen to open it and when she did, a man was standing there with a gun pointed at her. She told us all to run and hide, so we ran into my sister's bedroom and climbed under her bed. There was an almost-exhilaratingly hot fear in my body as I lay there looking out from under the bed skirt and listening to my mom talk to this man at the door. It felt similar to the fear I had at seeing my uncle on the hood of my mother's car that day, but this time I didn't cry. My sister was six years older than I was and she was sobbing. My brother was too. But I didn't cry at all. It was more of a curious fear that I was experiencing. It was as though I were outside of my own body and watching myself, controlling myself from the outside.

Much later, we learned that the man who had pointed the gun at my mom was not there to rob us, but had come to collect a debt that my dad owed him. The man worked for a loan shark whom my dad had borrowed money from and had failed to pay back (a habit of borrowing and trading and pawning that would haunt our family for the rest of our lives).

A few days after the incident, my mom and dad were in the grocery store when my mom saw the man who had pointed the gun at her. She told my dad.

"Bryan," she said, "that's him."

"What?"

"That's him. The man that came to our house."

My dad looked up, stared at the man in the aisle for a moment, then locked in his image as though he were looking through the scope of a gun or taking a picture of him.

"Wait here," he said.

My dad walked calmly out to their car and got his handgun from under the seat, tucked it in his pants, then walked back into the store. He scanned the aisles until he saw the man again and then he ran over to him and grabbed him by the collar of his shirt, put the gun to the man's head, and told him that if he ever threatened his family again, he would kill him. The other people in the store started screaming and running outside, and one of the cashiers called the police. My dad waited there in the store until the police came in and arrested him. Shortly after that incident, he decided to move us all from New Orleans to a small town called Covington, Louisiana, where he rented a small brick house just off of Highway 21.

4.

Times were tough. Since my mom's family still lived in New Orleans, and my dad's family lived in Chalmette, we were basically on our own now, even though we were only about an hour's drive away. My dad was still an electrician and had a large, baby blue van for his work, but we didn't have a second car anymore. The boat was gone too. When my brother and I started school the next year, my dad had to rent a car for my mom to be able to drive us back and forth.

The car we rented was a gray Pinto and my brother and I would ride in the trunk-like compartment in the back of the car. On cold mornings, we used our fingers to draw pictures on the slanted glass windshield, which was only inches above our faces.

One Saturday afternoon, my dad and brother and I were out in the front yard of our new house. My dad was building a cage for my older sister's rabbits, and my brother and I were playing in the leaves. My mom and sister were at the store. Suddenly, we heard my father cry out.

"Oh, boys!" he screamed.

We looked up from the pile of leaves we were rolling around in.

"Y'all run across the street and get some help."

We looked over at my dad, who seemed to be in pain. His face was red and he was squinting his eyes and gritting his teeth. We could see that he had somehow nailed one of his hands to the side of the rabbit cage that he was building. Blood was running down his dark, hairy arm.

"Hurry up," he said.

My brother and I ran across the street to an apartment complex, where an older couple let us inside their apartment. The husband went across the street and helped my dad pry his hand from the rabbit cage, then took him to the hospital. The old woman sat us down at her kitchen table and fed us candy for what seemed like a couple of hours until my mom and sister came home from the store. They both looked surprised and confused to see my brother and me playing next door, my dad nowhere in sight.

Eventually we went to the hospital and picked up my dad, and until he died years later, he never got rid of (and continued to wear) the green scrub shirt they gave him there in the ER. Maybe he thought it made him look like a doctor. (He would often dress in a dark black suit, wanting people to think he was a lawyer or a businessman. I think he was a very intelligent man, but without a high school diploma and with his blue collar background (his father and brothers were electricians, too), he never seemed satisfied with his place in life. He was always restless. I think that's why he drank. I also think that's how he was able to talk my mother into giving away custody of me to him. She could relate to something in his restless nature and perhaps there was more there, too. (I often think my middle name, Brian, though a variation on the spelling, was my mother's way of naming me after him. She often developed odd crushes on men and would become very flirtatious and inappropriate with them—in this case, her younger sister's husband.)

As money became scarcer and stranger things began happening, it was clear that my dad's problems with alcohol were worsening, even though this was just the beginning. How else could you explain someone nailing his hand to the side of a rabbit cage?

5.

We lived at that little rented house in Covington for only a year or so before moving into a rented trailer in Folsom, which was a smaller town further north. After a couple of years living there, we finally bought our own trailer and placed it on a piece of my grandfather's property, which was also in Folsom.

The piece of land was about twenty-two acres and was encircled by thick pine woods. A steep hill led down into a gulley, then rose again to a flat piece of land where we started to clear the spot for our trailer to go on. It was summer, and it was unbearably hot outside as we picked up sticks and trash to throw onto the fire while my dad chopped down trees and weeds with a machete.

It was slow work, a painful way for a ten-year-old boy to spend his summer, but the labor was broken up after a clay driveway was finally laid down and covered with white, dusty gravel. This allowed me and my brother to ride our bikes down the steep hill when we were finished picking up sticks and trash for the day. We spent the rest of our free time exploring the woods and the large horse farm just beyond the property. My dad would often take us to get thin cheeseburgers at the Jr. Food Mart in the center of town, which consisted of one red light, two gas stations, a grocery store, and a hardware store. This was all during the summer after fifth grade, which was the year after one of the worst school years of my life.

When I was in the fourth grade, I had a teacher named

Mrs. Theriot. It was the first time I had a teacher who, for whatever reasons, disliked me. Before that, I had always excelled in school. Being in school was the only time I felt in control of my life, where I had any control over how others felt about and perceived me. I didn't feel like "the adopted one" or "that crazy woman's son." I was a star pupil. I made straight As, read above my grade level, excelled in writing and reading, and in art. My first-grade teacher often talked about how she wished she had a "whole class full of Davids." So I was surprised when I got into the fourth grade and received little-to-no praise for my efforts.

Mrs. Theriot was downright cruel. Often she would tell us that she "didn't feel like teaching" and she would take the class outside to the playground, where we would play unsupervised for hours while she slept on one of the metal benches next to the baseball diamond. Something was wrong, but we, as kids, didn't know what it was. I'm amazed that no other adult at the school noticed this behavior and reported it. If they did, nothing was ever done by the administration. I remember telling my mom about some of this, but she didn't really know what to do about it at the time, either. My dad had stopped coming home on most nights by this point, and I think my mom was overwhelmed by raising three kids in a small trailer with a husband whose alcohol problem was becoming more and more serious every day.

Toward the middle of the school year, Mrs. Theriot had singled me out, along with a group of three or four other boys, as someone she was going to teach a lesson to. She started making evening phone calls to all our houses, telling our parents lies about how terrible we were in school. When she called my house, she told my mom that I was picking on other kids and stealing their lunch money (something I've never done, and pretty unoriginal on her part, really), but since my mom knew better, and since I had told her about this teacher, she just brushed off the phone call, and I was never in trouble at home because of it.

Once though, on a rare occasion when my dad was home, probably drunk, Mrs. Theriot called again. My dad answered the phone. I was at the kitchen table right beside him, doing my homework, and I wasn't paying much attention to the conversation he was having. I thought he was talking to my grandmother. After a few minutes, when he got off the phone, he looked at me and asked me if I knew who that was.

He had a strange grin on his face, so I smiled too, thinking he was going to tell me something pleasant.

"No?" I said. "Who was it?"

His alcohol-reddened face straightened out and his eyes instantly took on the almost-black color that they got when he was in a drunken rage. He took the back of his thick hand and smacked me across the side of my head. Hard. I almost fell off of the stool I was sitting on. I could feel the side of my face and my ear turning red from the heat of his hand.

"That was your teacher, Jack."

My dad had different names for us depending on how pissed off he was: Cap—short for captain, Babe—he called everyone, male or female—even his own mother—this, regardless of whether he was pissed off or not, Son—though he never *once* called me that; whether it was conscious on his part or not, I was always aware of that fact, Pod-nuh—his variation on partner, and Jack—reserved, it seemed, for his most violent anger.

I knew I was about to get it. There was no reasoning with him.

My dad hovered over me, and spit flew out of his mouth as he retold, in disgust, how my teacher told him that I was a bully who stole lunch money from other kids and never did my work in class. It was pretty much the same spiel that she had given my mom, only this time, it worked. That my dad could so readily believe this about me told me two things: that he didn't know me at all as a person, which made me mad, and that he was just so generally pissed off that he was *looking* for a reason to punish me.

He smacked me around good, pulled on my shirt, and tried some intimidating body language, but didn't draw blood or leave bruises, but it still hurt. It hurt my feelings, which I've learned is worse than any physical hurt. Those emotional bruises we acquire over the course of our lives never go away. My dad then set my punishment at nine weeks—the length of time until our next report cards came out—during which I would come home from school each day, go to my room, and "study" until it was time for dinner. After dinner, I would take a bath and go to bed. Every night. No exceptions.

On the weekends, I was to sit in my room all day and study. No TV, no Nintendo, no talking to my brother. Nothing. And my dad stuck to it. He never let me off early for good behavior, as they often do when you're older and wind up in prison. I served out my full sentence. And let me tell you, nine weeks is an awfully long time when you're ten years old.

Mrs. Theriot wasn't finished with us, though. One day she decided that we were all so beyond her help that we needed something really shocking to get us on the right path. She wanted to scare the living hell out of us. She told us that she was going to take our entire class to the parish jail for a field trip so that we "could see where we were headed if we didn't change our ways soon."

Some of the kids were scared, some excited, some just glad to get a day out of the classroom. I was petrified. Not because I was afraid of visiting a jail, not because I believed I would end up there one day, but because at the time she had scheduled the field trip, my dad was actually incarcerated there for a DWI and driving without a license. He was often in jail for things like that, and it was usually a relief when he was away from the house, as things tended to loosen up a bit with him gone, and the tension left our house like a draft of cold air. But I was horrified by the prospect of seeing him there, having my friends see him there. I knew if I stayed home that day and my friends saw him, I would never hear the end of it. I knew that my only chance was to go on the field trip and try to shield my friends from wherever my dad might have been kept in the jail. I prayed they wouldn't see him.

My mom cried when I came home from school that day and told her about it. I think the stress was piling up piece by piece and she didn't know what to do. Later, she actually called the jail and told them about our dilemma. The guards were very sympathetic, even apologizing to her, and promised they would hide my dad somewhere while the kids came through on the field trip. We went, and no one (not even me) saw my dad there. He later said that he just lay in his bunk all day with the covers pulled over his head, even though they had moved him to another cell where the group of fourth graders wasn't expected to pass.

A few months later, my family and I were at a Mardi Gras parade in New Orleans and I saw Mrs. Theriot. She was drunk and trying to hold herself up on one of the yellow police barricades. When she saw me, she started coming toward me and calling out my name.

"*Daaaaviiiddd!! Heeeeeeyyyyy, baaabbbyyyy!!!*" she yelled. A man was standing behind her and trying to hold her back from coming after me. She had a huge Styrofoam daiquiri cup in her hand and her large chest was covered with plastic Mardi Gras beads.

My parents sort of pulled me and my brother and sister away from her and we kept walking.

"Who the hell was that?" my dad asked. Of course, he had never been to my school before so he didn't know what my teacher even looked like.

"That was David's teacher," my mom said. "The one you talked to on the phone, remember?"

My mom knew the teacher had been lying, of course, and I heard her and my dad fighting a great deal over the punishment I received for that phone call, but my dad had stuck to his guns. Now I could see a revelation crossing his face. He knew then that this drunken woman had lied to him about me. But he never did say that he was sorry. He just looked at me, kind of pitifully, then back up at Mrs. Theriot.

"Come on, babe," he said. "Let's go."

The next year, when I was in fifth grade, we heard that Mrs. Theriot had died in a car accident. She had been drinking, and she had run off the road into a tree.

6.

For a short time, my dad had a shrimp boat which he kept near his parents' house in Chalmette. He had decided to give up being an electrician, working for his father and brothers, and to try to see if he could make a living as a shrimper. He was never home much at all during this time. He may have been staying with his parents or one of his brothers in Chalmette to be close to his boat, and it was probably only a few months that he actually did this sort of work—I don't think he was ever able to earn enough money to make it worth his while.

My father never really spent much quality time with me or my brother. There was a small handful of occasions during which he took us hunting or fishing, a couple of times where he tossed a baseball or football around with us in the backyard, when he taught us how to drive a Go-Kart he got for us one year. But inevitably, these moments would always end with either me or my brother, or both of us, getting punished and my dad leaving us kneeling on the concrete carport outside. We would then watch him get in his van and leave, my mom eventually having to come outside in order to relieve us from our forced act of contrition, which was being served for some unknown offense we had caused.

My dad had a sadistic sense of humor, too. His idea of playing with us involved him sitting on the trampoline in the backyard and throwing a tennis ball at us as we circled the trampoline and tried to climb up. It was like a twisted version of "King of the Hill." The goal of this game was simply to get on the trampoline without getting clobbered by the ball. My dad would laugh almost maniacally as he pegged us with the ball, and even though I was scared of getting hit, I was more scared of what he would do if I did *not* play. There was nothing more despicable to my dad than a coward. I knew this firsthand, as I had once watched my brother in a fight at school without jumping in to help him. When I got home that evening, my dad literally ripped the shirt off of my body as he pulled me toward him and spat in my face. His solution to handling bullies at school, which I experienced my share of, for sure, was to try to teach me how to box. He told me that if I didn't beat the shit out of any kid who picked on me that he would beat the shit out of me when I got home.

One time when we were playing this game with the tennis ball on the trampoline, my dad threw the ball so hard at my stomach that it knocked the wind out of me. I watched through my blurred sight as my dad straightened up from where he was crouching in the center of the trampoline. I saw the concern on his face as I tried to stumble toward him and catch my breath. Then I passed out.

When I woke up, he was standing over me and asking me if I was all right. I was, and even if I hadn't been, I probably wouldn't have told him. You had to act like a hardass around my dad all the time. Any sign of weakness was an opening for him to attack. You learned that quickly.

One morning, when it was still dark outside, my dad came into our room and woke us up. I was probably eight or nine years old. We knew that he was taking us out on his shrimp boat that day, and so we were already dressed and ready to go. We drove across the Causeway, the sun slicing up over the horizon of Lake Pontchartrain, the sky turning orange, then violet. My dad was chain-smoking Marlboro cigarettes and drinking coffee from a 32-ounce Time Saver thermos. He didn't have a radio in his little Mazda pickup. Since he had sold his blue work van to buy the shrimp boat, we rode in almost complete silence. There was always a thick tension in the air when it was just my dad, my brother, and me, and none of us seemed to know what to do to break through it.

When we pulled into the oyster-shell parking lot at the boat launch in Chalmette, I could smell fish, burning oil from the boat motors, and exhaust. Men were walking around in hip boots, smoking, drinking coffee, and country music came from some of the other trucks in the parking lot. We walked over to my dad's boat, a white-and-green shrimper with long metal booms coming from the sides and large green trawling nets folded up along the arms. The steering wheel was mounted on a sort of wooden column and there was a small windshield on top of that. Everything else was exposed to the elements.

My dad didn't let us drive the boat and it wasn't long before my brother and I were both pretty bored. At some point in the afternoon, after riding around on the water for a good while, the nets still empty, my dad stopped at a little fueling station that seemed to be floating between a bunch of tar-covered pilings in the middle of the dark water. The stubs of piling that stuck up above the dock were capped off with tin coverings held on with ten penny nails. The tin caps were dented and you could see cigarette butts and bird droppings in the crevices. We docked next to one of the gas pumps and got out, and my dad told us that he would get us something to drink when we got inside.

We followed him, walking over the wooden planks, which were wet and slick, and then we went in the small store. There was a bar alongside one of the walls with a bunch of men sitting on the metal stools. They were drinking beer and watching the little TV set that was above the bar. My brother and I dutifully followed our dad back to the cooler, where we each got a bottle of Barq's root beer and he got a tall can of Budweiser. When we went to put it on the counter, I suddenly had the urge to use the bathroom. I had seen a bathroom door between the coolers so maybe that's what put the notion in my head, but either way, I had to go real bad all of a sudden.

My dad was telling us to put our root beers on the counter so he could pay, then he told us to sit down on the stools and wait for him to come back. He said he was going to use the bathroom. I thought this would be a good time to go myself, and so I followed him toward the little brown door that said MEN.

Seeing me behind him, my dad turned around and looked at me.

"You don't need to follow me in here," he said. "Get your ass back over there. I'll be out in a minute."

He laughed and shook his head as he went in the bathroom, the door closing behind him. Something on his face seemed to say that he was embarrassed that I was "following him," but what he didn't know and what I was too afraid to tell him was that I had to go too. I mean really, really go.

But I tried to hold it in. I walked back to the bar, as I had been told to do, and sat down on one of the stools, thinking that sitting down would help. It did, but after just a minute, my dad was coming out of the bathroom and telling us to come on. It was time to go. It was my last chance to tell him I had to go to the bathroom too, but I chickened out. I was just too scared that I'd get in trouble.

So we left and I hadn't asked to go to the bathroom.

When we got back on the boat, the urge to go was worse. All I could think about was how badly I had to go. It seemed as if we were hours away from getting back to the launch, and so I tried to sit down on one of the thwarts to keep from going all over myself. It didn't help. The boat was cutting through the rough water and we were rocking from side to side and I just couldn't hold it any longer. I got up and stood at the back of the boat and relieved myself, quietly, in my jeans.

I could feel it going down my leg, but it was too late to stop now. When I finished, I felt a lot better physically, but mentally the reality was starting to hit me. I didn't know what I was going to do.

Luckily, the wind from the moving boat kept anyone from noticing what I had done, and my pants held everything in pretty good, but when we got to the launch and climbed out of the boat, I knew that I was in trouble. While my dad and brother started to get the ice chests and whatever else we had from the boat and were putting it in the back of the truck, I walked across the oyster-shell lot and looked for something to clean myself off with. The only thing I found was a dirty, dried-up old rag that was half-buried under some dirt and rocks. I picked this up and hid behind a Dumpster and tried to wipe my legs and the inside of my pants. The stiff rag didn't do much good to clean me off, but I was in better shape than before at least. That was all I could do except for just hoping that I could make it back home without my dad noticing what I had done.

We climbed into the cab of the small pickup truck. There was just a bench seat inside so one of us had to sit in the middle next to the gear shift and since it was cold outside, all the windows were rolled up. My dad didn't even start the truck before he knew what I had done. He wasn't mad, like I thought he'd be, probably disturbed, maybe even sad that I would resort to such a thing. Definitely he was disgusted. I was nine or ten years old, for God's sake. I don't know if he really spent much time thinking about that or not. But he made me get out of the cab and sit in the open bed of the truck among the ice chests and fishing tackle.

It was cold back there as we rode along the interstate so I pulled some of the ice chests around me so that I was in a sort of fort. Occasionally, I would see my dad look out the back window of the cab and, at some point, I actually saw him laughing at me. My brother was laughing too, but I think it was more just to stay in good with my dad. I never held that against him. You did what you had to do. I sat there in the cold and waited until we got home. Thankfully, we were going to my grandmother's house in New Orleans so I wouldn't have to sit back there for the near two hours it would've taken to get back to our trailer in Folsom.

When we finally got to the house, my dad told my brother to go inside. He told me to stand in the driveway and take off all of my clothes. I looked at him in shock.

"Well, you sure as hell ain't goin' in your grandma's house like that," he said.

I looked out at the street, mortified by the cars passing by in both directions. There was nothing to hide me from the traffic, the neighbors.

"Go ahead, take 'em off."

My dad was walking over to the side of the house now, reaching for the garden hose and turning on the spigot. I pulled my clothes off and stood completely naked in the driveway. I was cold. I was pale and skinny and embarrassed. Cars passed by. The people inside of the cars looked out at me. Saw me naked, probably wondered what was going on here. I closed my eyes as my dad sprayed the icy water on my body, cleaning me off. I hated him more than I had hated anyone else in my life up until that moment. I hated myself too. I wished that I would die.

As I was being sprayed off, my mom came outside on the

front porch (she was there visiting, and me and my brother were supposed to ride back home to Folsom with her).

"Bryan," she said. "What are y'all doing? It's freezing out here."

I looked down at the cold driveway, the streams of dirty water running down toward the gutter in the street, and I started preparing myself for the next round of humiliation: my dad telling her what I had done, the inevitable look of confusion and disappointment crossing over her face.

"He fell in the mud, babe," my dad said. "Get back inside. We'll be in in a minute."

"How did that happen?" she said.

"I don't know, babe, he just fell. What do you want me to do? Why don't you go inside and fill up the tub so he can take a bath?"

My mom just shook her head. She bought it.

"Okay," she said. Then she walked back inside the house and closed the door behind her.

I couldn't look at my dad, so I kept looking down at the driveway as he finished spraying me off with the hose.

"All right," he said. "Go inside and take you a bath."

He handed me a towel and I wrapped it around myself and walked inside. To this day, I don't know if he ever told my mom what really happened, or if he somehow felt responsible for it—that he had created such a culture of fear in our house that it had escalated to the point where I was afraid to ask to use the bathroom. That I would rather shit myself than ask for permission to sit on a toilet.

Another time when the toilet in the bathroom that my brother and I shared was broken, my dad instructed us to use the toilet in his and my mom's bathroom. I woke up in the middle of the night once and had to go so terribly, but was afraid to walk through my parents' bedroom to use their toilet, so I used my brother's and mine anyway. My dad had said that we couldn't flush the toilet in there because he wanted the insulation under the trailer to dry out before he could get under the house to see what the problem was with the plumbing, so I didn't flush. Instead I climbed in my bed after I finished, and I prayed that the toilet would just empty itself out somehow. That God would do it for me. I prayed about this every day that week. I prayed until the weekend when my dad would go into the bathroom to work on the problem and, of course, discover that I had used the toilet anyway, not even bothering to flush it. He was appalled, I could tell. But I think he was more disturbed, though, that I again had been more fearful of *him* and what he might do to me if I walked through his bedroom in the middle of the night to use the bathroom that I would rather use the broken toilet and not flush it—because of that, presumably, he never yelled at me or punished me for it. He just flushed the toilet himself, shaking his head in a sort of disbelief, and waited until the next weekend to work on it. Maybe he was glad he had an extra week before having to climb under the damp, dark trailer, the insulation hanging down in itching pink clumps, the mud under his back and the dogs licking his face as he tried to work on the leaking plastic pipes. Maybe he was just sad that I was so scared of him, that I would never really feel at home in his house. Maybe he didn't think about any of that at all, I don't know. But it was those moments, and others like it, that helped to set up one of the great paradoxes of the man I called "Dad." How he could be so mean and violent one minute, only to sweep you over with a stroke of pure human compassion and forgiveness the next.

7.

I've often wondered about my dad's mental state and whether or not his alcoholism contributed to it or was more a *result of it*. As I grew up, he seemed to deteriorate, growing angrier, more violent, more paranoid. When I was still about nine or ten years old, he started to tell my brother and me that he owed the IRS a great deal of money (which was true), and that they were likely going to show up at our house one day and "clean us out." That meant, he told us, that they would take our furniture, our clothes, even our toys. He suggested that if there was anything we cared a great deal about and that we didn't wish to lose that we should hide it really good.

I can remember stuffing some of my favorite G.I. Joe toys into the floor vents of my room in our trailer. Even after being warned to never put anything in there, as it could cause a fire, the risk of that paled next to the thought of some suited men (that's how I pictured them in my mind) coming into our house and taking all of our belongings. The sad thing about this was that my dad told us that story in complete earnestness—there was no anger, no worry, really, in his voice, just a sort of sad resignation of this new reality we were being faced with. He completely believed what he was telling us. And after witnessing the meter man from the electric company in our backyard on more than one occasion—his hand on the switch to cut our power for non-payment, my mom begging him, crying for him not to turn our power off, that she had three kids in school, that she would pay the bill tomorrow, only to have the switch turned off anyway, the man pulling away in his truck and leaving us in the dark—I believed my dad about this too.

Years later, he would start thinking that the mafia had tapped our telephones. He told us to be extremely careful about what we said. As a child and even as a preteen, you're usually groomed to believe your parents, whatever they say, and this, at the time, seemed completely plausible too. I remember spending many nights and days being terrified of the IRS, the police, the mafia. Fortunately, none of this came to fruition. At least not quite how my dad told us it would.

My dad's fear of and disdain for the police was not altogether unfounded, though. He had had numerous incidents with the local cops, and being that there were only three or four officers in the small town of Folsom where we lived, my dad was an easy and a very recognizable target. Almost every time they spotted his little tan Mazda pickup truck, they would pull him over, slam his face against the steaming hood, and hold him there while they searched the cab. I can still remember seeing the bright burn marks on my dad's face one time when they released him from jail. Inevitably, they would find a gun under his seat, since he always carried one—illegally, no less, since he never had a permit for it; on top of that, they would get him for driving without a license. His license had been suspended and revoked so many times that he simply stopped trying to get one.

Once I was in the truck with him, along with my brother and grandfather, when the police pulled him over. Within five minutes, my dad was in the back of the police cruiser, and they were taking him away. I suppose they didn't want to make a scene with us as witnesses, but it was still traumatic to see how quickly it all happened. It didn't seem as though they said anything to him at all. It was as if they had been waiting for him to pass by, then grabbed him from the road like wolves after a deer.

Not long after that, my dad was driving home on one of the narrow back roads in Folsom when he flipped his truck into the ditch. He was drunk, not wearing a seat belt, and his head went right through the windshield. Since it was late at

39

night and dark back there on the country road, no one found him, no one passed by to see the brake lights coming up from the ditch, to hear the horn honking into the muddy grass. Eventually my dad regained consciousness, climbed out of the truck by himself, and walked to a nearby house. Upon seeing his bloody face, the homeowners let him stay on the porch while they called 911. But instead of taking him to the hospital, the police, upon recognizing who my dad was and the state he was in (they could probably smell the beer on his clothes), took him straight to jail.

Weeks later, when my brother and I were snooping around the wreckage that was now parked in a shed behind our trailer, I found a pencil that had gone through my dad's chin during the wreck (he had told us about pulling it out of his face before climbing from the crashed truck). The sharp end of the pencil was clean, but oddly the flat end with the eraser was caked with dried, dark blood. There was at least an inch of dried, brownish-red blood on the shaft of the pencil, indicating that it had gone that far into my dad's face. I'll never forget that the white pencil had words etched in blue along its side: it said JESUS LOVES YOU.

My dad tried his best to be a good father, I think. I have fond memories of him teaching us how to ride the Go-Kart he bought for us one year. I can remember him helping my brother and me tie our scooters to the back of his truck with strands of long yellow rope and pulling us around in the large field behind our trailer. It was probably one of the most fun things I ever did as a child, like water-skiing only with no boat and no water. He taught me how to shoot my .410, and took us hunting for dove and squirrel a handful of times. It seemed, though, that he was cursed with bad luck. We always either got lost in the woods, ran out of gas on our boat, got our lines tangled with some branches near the bank of whatever body of water we were on, or something. It always ended badly, with my dad getting mad and throwing things, yelling at me and my brother for something we had done wrong, as if we were supposed to automatically know how to do these things that he had never taught us before.

Once we were hunting dove on our property in Folsom, where we had just moved our new trailer. The land was mostly wooded then, only a small clearing where we lived and the path where the gravel driveway cut through. My brother, my dad and I were sitting in the leaves, leaning against a pine tree and looking across the hilly land that my dad had illegally seeded, waiting for some birds to shoot at. To this day, I don't know if my dad did this on purpose or not, but at some point he looked down at me and he whispered for me to look up toward the top of a large oak, where a huge bird stood perched in one of the branches. He told me that I should shoot it.

"Is that a dove?" I asked him.

"Yeah, babe, it's just a big one."

I looked at the large bird for a good while. I raised my gun and sighted it with the bead at the end of the black barrel. The bird was still save for a couple of rufflings of its wings and a few twitches of its head. I couldn't really tell what kind of bird it was. I also didn't want to disappoint or disobey my dad, so I decided to take the shot, expecting that I would just miss anyway, the bird flying off into the woods somewhere at the sound of the shotgun blast. I squeezed the trigger. But I didn't miss the bird. I could hear it thumping down against the branches as it pirouetted out of the tree. When it flopped on the leafy ground I walked over to it and could immediately tell that this was not a quail. Or a dove. It wasn't anything I was supposed to shoot. It was a hawk.

"Shit," my dad said, coming up behind me to look down at what I had just killed. You could see the blood on the animal's beak, and its tiny black eyes stared straight up at me as though it were shaming me for what I had just done to it. Its wings were folded peacefully against its gray body as it lay in the dirt. My dad didn't seem mad, though, which was good, but I didn't know what was going to happen now that I had really killed this thing.

"That's illegal what you just did, you know?" he said.

I didn't say anything. My heart was racing. My stomach ached. I was scared that the police or the game warden would come from some hiding spot in the woods and that they would take me to a juvenile detention center.

Sensing this fear, my dad started to laugh. He always seemed to take some sort of sadistic joy from others' pain or worry. I'll never know why. He told me not to worry about it, though, that we would take the hawk home with us and that maybe he would have it mounted for me. It wouldn't go to waste, he said. He promised that.

But when we got home and he told my mom what I had done, she looked at me like I had seen her look at me so many times before during my young life: it was a look of disdain, disgust, worry, and utter confusion at the budding sociopath she seemed to think I was. She insisted I had killed the hawk intentionally, even after my dad took the heat for it, said that he told me to shoot it, that I didn't know it was a hawk, that he hadn't known either. My mom just started crying, though, told me she couldn't believe I would do such a thing, and then she sent me to my room and told me not to let her see my face for the rest of the day.

I'm sure that her and my dad fought about this, and I know that he told her over and over that it was an accident, but she never would accept that. In her head, I had moved up from killing insects to killing protected species of birds. What would be next? I know she often watched me closely and how I treated my brother. What would probably be considered normal spats between siblings were great cause for concern on her part. I remember quite a few talks about my temper and how if I ever put a hand on my brother again I would be in serious trouble. I used to feel as though I were being threatened that I would be kicked out of the house, sent into foster care or some such thing. That I was unwanted. And because of this, my place there always felt tenuous, like I was a boarder or a temporary guest who had outstayed his welcome. I was always ready to leave, never really felt entitled to my place in the world or with my basic human needs. This feeling has followed me throughout my entire life.

I think I scared my parents, both of them, even my dad, who was such a hardass. But I don't think either one of them will ever know the deep remorse I felt for shooting that hawk, the pain it caused me, and the hurt of knowing that my mom thought I did it on purpose, that I was somehow a bad person. Evil. My dad never did get the hawk mounted for me as he had promised to do. Not that I would've wanted that bird's hollow eye staring down at me all the time, reminding me of how much I fucked everything up.

8.

A few years after that my dad wanted to take us duck hunting at a camp in Dulac, Louisiana. The camp belonged to a friend of his from work, and the guy had invited us to go spend the weekend out there. The only problem was that I had broken my arm a couple of weeks before trying to lift my brother up into his bunk bed, which was on top of mine, and the doctor had put a cast going all the way up to my shoulder, told me I had to wear it like that until the bone mended, probably about six weeks.

My dad really wanted me and my brother to go hunting with him, though. He was determined. That's just how he was:

he would get his mind set on something despite how impractical it may have been and he would not relent in his pursuit of it. The thing was that he had never really been consistent in taking my brother and me hunting or fishing. He would take us to do these things on occasion, but it would almost always end badly. This time was somewhat of an exception, though.

My brother and I each had a .410 that my dad had given us and had shown us how to shoot. We had some paper targets in the backyard with giant bucks and quail and squirrels painted on them and we would tear these up with our shotguns. I was still pretty young and the butt of the gun bruised my shoulder when I shot it.

There was no way, my dad said, that I could go hunting with a broken arm. I didn't really care. I just told him I'd stay home. Waking up at 4 a.m. and riding out in the cold marsh and getting wet standing in a blind wasn't exactly how I wanted to spend my Christmas break anyway, so I took my broken arm and the cast around it as a sort of blessing. But my dad was absolutely determined to do this thing. He said that I didn't really need the cast going all the way up to my shoulder like that anyway. I had broken my wrist, so having the cast any higher than my elbow was just pointless, he said.

My mom told him that the doctor probably had a very good reason for setting the cast like that, and that it was probably a bad idea to mess around with it. It was as though my dad didn't hear her though. I knew better than to say anything, so when he came inside the trailer with a hacksaw one night, I stayed quiet to see if he was seriously thinking about doing what I thought he was going to do.

"Come here, babe," he said.

I got up from the floor where I was lying down watching TV and followed him into the kitchen.

"Bryan, what are you doing?" my mom asked him.

"I told you, babe, I'm going to take the boys hunting, and

Dave can't go with this cast all the way up to his elbow like this. I'm gonna just cut some of it off."

I stood next to the kitchen table, where my dad had already placed the hacksaw, his black plastic ashtray with a burning cigarette leaning out of it, and his glass of beer. Then I waited to see where this would go.

"Come on, babe," my dad said again. "I'm not gonna hurt you. Sit down."

I looked over at my mom, who had apparently decided not to throw her hat in the ring on this one, and then I sat down at the kitchen table and put my broken arm on top of it. My dad pushed his beer out of the way, picked up his cigarette and put it between his lips, took a long drag from it, then put it back in the ashtray. His arms and chest were dark and hairy and I could see and hear how heavily he was breathing.

As he picked up the hacksaw and brought the serrated blade down to the fiberglass cast, I could see his hand quivering. I knew it wasn't because he was scared about doing this, or nervous, but that his hands just always shook like that. When he spooned cough medicine into our mouths when we were much younger, a lot of the syrup would drop out of the spoon onto the floor, such was the shaking of his hands. It must've been the alcohol.

My dad placed the blade right below the point where my elbow was and where the cast started to curve, holding my arm in a natural sling position.

"You ready?" he said.

"Uh-huh."

I still wasn't sure if he was serious or not. I was unsure because once when I was probably about six years old, I had a loose tooth that just wouldn't fall out on its own. I pulled on it and played with it, ate Now & Later candies, all to no avail. The tooth just wouldn't come out. My dad had told me that the only way to get it out was to tie my tooth to the doorknob on the front door and let him slam the door shut. When this happened, it would yank that damned tooth right out, he said. I was terrified by this prospect, but even more terrified of telling my dad that I was terrified, so I let him tie a string around my loose tooth, then run the string a couple of feet until he had enough slack to wrap it around the doorknob. I was literally shaking with fear. He started to move the door on its hinges, very slowly, as though he were testing it out, getting it ready. I clenched my fists, trying to keep the tears from spilling out from my eyes when I closed them.

"You ready?" he said.

I nodded. I waited for the sound of the door slamming, the sound of skin tearing as the final threads of nerve or whatever was holding my tooth in place after all this time tore loose. A few seconds went by. Then a couple more. I opened my eyes slowly and could see my dad still standing by the front door, holding on to it and laughing in that deep, sadistic way that he had. His face would turn red, spit would form at the corners of his mouth, and his lips would pull taut. It was as though it pained him to laugh so he held it mostly in but you could still see the pleasure he got from watching one of us suffer his jokes.

So it was with that thought that I nodded, telling him that I was ready for him to start hacking away at my arm, still not really sure if he was going to do it or not. But then I heard the sound of the rusty metal blade tearing into the fiberglass and I could feel the dust from it coming up into my nose and powdering my eyes.

"Hold still," he said. He repositioned my arm on the table and kept sawing. My mom was standing by the kitchen sink and just watching all of this as though it were on TV and not happening right there in her kitchen like that.

The blade had started to cut through the cast and was tearing at the material beneath it now. The serrated edges of the blade got hung up several times on the material and my dad had to pull the saw away and then tear at the fabric with his fingers. He stopped every now and then to take a drag from his cigarette or to drink from his glass of beer. His face was red and I could tell he was drunk. I just kept hoping that he wouldn't cut my arm.

He brought the blade back down and now he was going around the circumference of the cast. I had to hold my arm in very uncomfortable positions (which were made even more uncomfortable by the fact that my bone was broken and trying to heal) as he sawed away. When he got through the cast and most of the material underneath it, I started to move my arm into a more manageable position. That's when I felt the sharp edge of that rusty blade tear into my arm. It didn't cut deep, but it cut just enough for me to bleed, and the dirty blade made it burn more than it probably should have.

I sucked in air through my teeth to let him know that he had cut me. I didn't want to say "oww" or anything that he might perceive as weak.

"You all right, babe?" he said.

"Yeah, I just got cut a little."

He looked at my forearm where the blood was starting to trickle down into the cast now.

"You'll be all right," he said.

Then he took some sharp scissors and cut the cotton wrapping that covered my skin, dabbing at the cut with it to soak up some of the blood. The bloodied cotton came off in long wispy strands, like spider webs, and my arm underneath was pale and looked much skinnier than my other arm. It felt heavier, though. It was as if I had just woken up from sleeping on it all night.

The cast and the under-wrapping were now in two halves. My dad picked up the saw again and sliced through the upper half until he had a crevice carved out all the way up to my shoulder. Once this was accomplished, he pried the top half apart with his thick fingers and he pulled it off. Then he took the scissors again and cut the tendrils of cotton and fabric away until I was left with a short cast going from my hand to my elbow. I could move my arm freely now but it still hurt very badly when I did so. This was my trigger hand too. I would have to press on the trigger of my shotgun with my index finger and hope that it didn't send a shard of pain up my wrist like it was doing right now.

"How's that feel?" my dad asked.

"Good," I lied.

"You think you can shoot now?"

"I should be able to."

"All right," he said. "Now we're talkin. Why don't you go get packed up? We're leaving tomorrow morning."

"Okay," I said.

"Early," he added.

As I got up and started walking back to my room, the pain throbbing in my arm, the little knick from the saw blade burning, I turned around and saw my dad toss the pieces of my cast and the long strands of cotton, sinewy and stubborn as horse hair, into the garbage can. Then he got up and took his beer and his ashtray into his room, shutting the door behind him. He left the rusty hack saw, now with a little bit of blood on it too, sitting on the kitchen table.

It seemed as though we had been barely sleeping for an hour when my dad came into our room and woke us up. It was still dark outside and even the air in our room felt cold and damp. My brother and I stumbled out of our beds and got dressed. My dad and my grandfather had taken us to an army surplus store a couple of days earlier and bought us some hip boots, thermal underwear, some large camouflaged suits that zipped up the front, a bunch of boxes of shotgun shells, and some duck calls. All of this was already packed in the truck and so we went outside into the cold.

The truck was parked in the gravel driveway and it was already running. The headlights were on and the windshield wipers were going even though it wasn't raining. You could see the little slivers of ice as the wipers broke them from the glass and knocked them onto the gravel. It was cold enough to see your breath in front of your face.

It took a couple of hours to drive down to the hunting camp. My brother and I slept most of the way but eventually woke up when the roads started to get bumpy with the oyster-shell surface that covered them. On both sides of the road were fields of cane and marsh grass, high enough so that you couldn't see over them from the cab of the truck. It was still dark outside and the headlights bounced over the road, making the shells in front of us appear almost perfectly white against the black sky overhead.

We drove over levees and down one-lane roads, my dad probably getting lost more than a few times, but never saying anything about where we were. It was always like that riding in my dad's truck—complete silence. There was no radio, he kept the window down only a crack since it was so cold outside, and the sound of gravel under the tires was muted by the soft mud we were driving over. My dad smoked and drank coffee from his Time Saver thermos and didn't say anything to us.

I could hear the train before I even saw any tracks. We were coming over a rise and then the cane was gone and I could see the circle of light coming toward us and the train behind it bellowing. It was a couple hundred yards off and there were no gates to come down to keep you from going over the tracks so my dad decided to gun it. I saw the look on his face as he pitched his cigarette out the window, the orange ashes raining down on the dark grass and then I saw his hand tighten around the steering wheel as he put the truck into third gear. The tires skidded against the shells and the mud but eventually they caught and we were going up the slope toward the track. The train was closer now, much closer, and it was getting louder and the light brighter as it started to fill the passenger window, which I was looking out of in mute shock.

The truck lurched over the track and the creosote-covered railroad ties like some wild horse and then we were on the other side, the train skimming behind the truck as it slid by us, barely missing total disaster, the cold metal cars covered with graffiti and the metal wheels screeching across the track like a nail over a chalkboard. I looked over at my dad, who still didn't say anything, but I could see a grin forming under his beard. He lit another cigarette and kept going down the road, slower now as the skeletons of the raised hunting camps started to come up over the marshgrass and cane, silhouetted against the sky, which was just now starting to gray with the coming morning.

When we finally pulled up to the camp, it was light outside but the camp itself was dark. There was no porchlight on, no lights illuminated the small windows. We got out of the truck and stretched, then went over to the house and opened the screen door. My dad knocked. No one answered. He went around and looked through a couple of the windows and came back and told us that no one was there yet. We were early, he said.

It was cold outside but my dad didn't want to run the truck anymore so we followed him around the camp and went down to the water where several flatboats were docked, bobbing up and down in the cold black water. You could walk across the wooden dock and go underneath the hunting camp, where there was a plywood counter and a stainless steel sink embedded in it. The water lapped up against the dock and it smelled stagnant, like something rotten and dead.

We made our way back up the embankment on the side of the camp and walked back over to the truck. My brother had to use the bathroom so my dad and I watched him walk over one of the muddy fields across the road and into the stands of cane. My dad had given him a roll of toilet paper to take back there with him and found the sight of his only biological son walking into the mud in the early morning cold with a roll of damp toilet paper hitting against his thigh something worth laughing at. I only had sympathy, as I'd been there before, but at least my brother had the courage to ask my dad to use the bathroom.

A while later, my dad's friend Roy pulled up in his truck and parked beside us. He had a couple of dogs in the back and the dogs were hanging out of the bed, looking as though at any minute one of them would leap out. Mr. Roy had his window rolled down and was laughing at us standing out in the cold. He stopped the truck and killed the engine. You could hear it clicking under the hood as it cooled off.

His son Carl was in the passenger side of the truck and he got out and started grabbing their guns and other gear from the bed. He looked a couple of years older than me, with a sweep of brown hair hanging down just over his eyes and pale skin. He was wearing his camouflage already but instead of boots he was wearing a pair of Reebok Pumps. I had coveted shoes like that since they first came out but my parents couldn't afford the forty-five dollar price tag and so I looked at this older boy with a bit of envy as he carelessly walked around in the mud with shoes I would've done almost anything to have. I immediately looked up to him.

Carl seemed to know exactly what he was doing as he unlocked the door to the camp and started taking stuff inside. I could tell that he had been out here before, probably ever since he was a little kid, and so none of this was new to him. I was nervous and apprehensive. My dad had shown me how to shoot my .410. We had practiced some more with it in the backyard after he cut my cast off. And while it hurt my arm to shoot, the pain was tolerable and so I didn't say anything about it. But still I had never been to a place like this before, had never killed a duck, and I wasn't very happy about being here now.

The inside of the camp was dusty and plain. Its walls were covered with brown wainscoting and single, dull light bulbs hung from little fixtures in the ceiling. Some of the fixtures had aluminum foil wrapped around them, presumably to throw off more light into the mostly dark room. Otherwise, none of the light bulbs were covered and the light they gave off was dim and yellow. The furniture looked like it had been cast off from some other house, and from some previous decade. It was also brown or yellow and made of uncomfortable fabric that itched your skin when you sat on it. Everything inside smelled musty and stale, as though fresh air hadn't seeped into this place in a long time.

There were three rooms that were identical inside. All of them were lined with gray steel bunk beds—three to each room—and the thick carpet was a dingy yellow color. A couple of the rooms had leaky window units jutting out of the small windows, some of them huffing out warm air into the already stale atmosphere. These windows were covered with tin foil so that the rooms inside were completely devoid of any natural light. Several prints hung on the walls—prints of marsh scenes, heroic-looking dogs retrieving limp birds from the water, silhouettes of hunters in the reeds. They were all generic, though, nothing personal or artistic about any of them. They were simply something to cover up the empty brown space on the walls. There was also a Budweiser clock glowing on a wall in the kitchen but other than that, there was nothing.

We put our duffel bags in one of the rooms, hung our shotguns on one of the gunracks in the den, then walked out onto the sagging porch that jutted out over the water. Across the canal you could see the marsh. It was gray and seemed to stretch on for miles. Everything here was flat and gray and quiet. My dad seemed to be in his element, though. There was a sense that the rules of the rest of the world didn't quite apply here. A sense that you could get away with much more than you could elsewhere. I think my dad picked up on this, perhaps he knew about it way before we came here, and this made him glad.

It was still early but my dad had already started drinking. Some other hunters began to arrive and they were sitting around the table in the den and smoking, drinking beer and whiskey, telling dirty jokes about women, saying things that I had never heard before. My brother and I sat on the flannel sofa and listened to them, just taking everything in.

After a while a few of the other men there started talking about going out on one of the boats to shoot some nutria. My dad told me and my brother that we had to stay at the camp but that he was going to go. When he got back, he said, we could practice shooting some skeet. He said we were going to have a good time.

There was a small TV hanging up in one of the corners of the den and so we watched that for a while: the TV seemed to get only one or two channels so we had to watch NASCAR or golf. We settled on watching the cars race around the tracks but soon that got boring and we went outside. We walked down the oyster-shell covered embankment and went over to the dock again. Now the flatboats were gone, as the men had taken both of them out into the water to kill nutria, and you could see the dead fish flapping up against the pilings. It was still cold outside.

I looked over underneath the camp and could see the older boy Carl kneeling in front of the wooden counter and petting one of the Catahoulas that his dad had brought along. I walked over there to pet the dog.

"What's his name?" I said.

"A-Dog," he said.

"Huh?"

"Yeah, my dad hates thinking up names for em so he just calls them A, B, C, D, and so on. It even says that on their papers."

I laughed, knowing that he wasn't kidding around, but somehow it just seemed like something I should laugh at. The boy laughed a little bit too and then went back to petting the dog. We didn't say anything else.

That night after we had all filled up on bowls of steaming jambalaya made from the nutria the men had killed that afternoon, someone had the idea to go shining on the levee road for rabbits. Shining is when you take a flashlight and point it at what you want to kill, blinding it, freezing the animal as still as a statue while its eyes adjust to the light, then shooting it before it has a chance to run. This is illegal in Louisiana, especially when you're doing it from a public road like we were planning to do.

My dad, my brother, Roy's son Carl, and I walked out from the camp and into the dark, each with a flashlight and a shotgun in his hands, and we went up the levee, from whose mounded surface you could see the dark skeletons of the raised camps against the navy blue sky behind them, the moonlight reflecting in shards against the canal and the marsh behind it.

We walked with our lights before us, the white beams bobbing up and down over the marshgrass until my dad stopped still.

"Look," he whispered. His flashlight's white beam was hovering over what looked to be a large cane-cutter. It was completely still in his quivering cone of light.

"Shoot him," he said, Carl immediately lifting up his twelve gauge and shooting, the echo spreading out over the marsh and making a sound similar to the loud clap of two sheets of plywood smacking into one another. The buckshot hit the shape outlined in the light, tiny holes pocking the black silhouette, but the shape didn't fall over or move. Instead it just kind of twitched, then regained its previous form. When we walked over to it, we saw that what my dad had thought was a rabbit—and which Carl had obliterated with his shotgun—was just a large bush. We all laughed, but there was something ominous, almost foreboding, about this. It would almost come to serve as a sort of precursor for the rest of the trip.

Later on when we were back at the camp and most of the men had gone to sleep, my brother and I stayed up with Carl and a couple of older kids who were drinking whiskey and beer, smoking, and playing cards. My brother and I didn't drink or smoke. We were too afraid my dad would come out and catch us. He had once told us that when he started smoking at nine years old, his father had caught him and punished him for six months. Much like when my dad would punish me or my brother later on in his life, his father didn't relent on the punishment. My dad was punished for the entire time, couldn't leave his room save for eating dinner, using the bathroom, or going to school. I never asked my dad if his punishment fell on any holidays, and if it had, if his father had let him off for that, at least. None of this strict discipline seemed to work on my dad, however. Unlike his older brother, who would later join the Marines and who always followed the rules to the letter, my dad was often referred to by his family as "the black sheep." He was the only one who ever moved away from "the Parish" where he was born and raised.

So despite his six-month punishment and I'm sure the physical beating that preceded it, my dad continued to smoke cigarettes out of his opened bedroom window, he told us, if for no other reason than to spite his father. My dad was into other mischief as a young boy as well. Once he told us about how he and some friends would go around the neighborhood and knock on people's doors—when the person answered, opening the door to him and his friends, they would toss water balloons into the house. Then they would run away, laughing. He told us about a time they were doing this and how one of his friends had, unbeknownst to him, filled one of the balloons with white paint. When the poor old lady whose door they knocked on finally answered, my dad's friend tossed the paint-filled balloon into the house. The other boys were too shocked to run, and as it turned out the old lady knew all of them anyway, knew their parents as well. My dad spent the next few months of his life earning money to pay for the damage.

Another thing he liked to do was tie two aluminum garbage cans together with a piece of thin white string. He and his friends (who were usually a lot older than he was) would then place each can on opposite sides of the street, then wait until a car passed, hitting the string and pulling the two cans into the car, one hitting each side and often making large dents in the doors. My dad would tell us these stories proudly, but never would put up with us doing anything even remotely resembling the things he had done. To this day, I'm not sure why he told us these things.

Nonetheless, my brother and I were both amply afraid of my dad so that we did not partake in the drinking and smoking that the other boys were doing—that would come later in both of our lives. I remember watching the older boys though with a sort of envy and admiration—how they seemed so comfortable being in this hunting camp, doing the things that their fathers did, destined to fill their shoes one day. This was the first time my dad had ever taken us to do anything like this, and neither my brother nor I knew what to do, what to expect. So we watched the older boys and tried to take their cue, but we just didn't touch any of the beer or whiskey or cigarettes. One of them finally went out to his dad's truck to listen to music, where he passed out, and then the rest of us went into our rooms, which were all filled with stagnant air and the grumbling of snoring men piled into the metal bunks. I climbed into mine and wrapped myself up in a thick brown blanket.

The next morning my dad woke us up early again. It was still dark outside and you could feel the cold in the air even though the heaters were on. We ate some scrambled eggs with Tabasco sauce on them and then we got dressed in our thermal underwear and camouflaged overalls. We put on our rubber waders, our gloves, dark knit hats, grabbed our shotguns, and went outside into the gray morning. Mr. Roy was already in one of the boats, its outboard humming, the exhaust coming out over the water, and the dogs running from bow to stern. He told us where to sit and once we were in the boat, he pulled away from the dock and then we were speeding down the wide canal, the cold air and water stinging our faces.

I kept my face tucked in my coat and tried to keep my cast dry too as we rode around in the marsh. At some point we came to a little berm where a bunch of pirogues were sitting in the grass and Mr. Roy pulled the boat up into the mud. We climbed into the pirogues in pairs and then Mr. Roy pulled us in a sort of caravan deeper into the marsh where the water was too shallow for his outboard. The sky was turning orange now and you could already see the black shapes of ducks flying against the flat horizon. We each started to untie our pirogues from the main boat and then we floated off to our blinds.

Time went by very slowly. We couldn't talk, couldn't move, and so we just sat in the cold, brown, sulfur-smelling water, smacking gnats from our necks and faces, and waiting for ducks. Eventually we shot a few, and when we went out in the pirogue to collect them, I could see that one of them was still alive, circling in the water. My dad got out from the little boat, the mud and water sucking at his waders, and picked up the dead ducks, tossed them inside the pirogue next to me, then went over to the duck that had not been killed and snapped its neck. Its weight when he tossed it into the hull of the boat sounded and felt like a wet beach towel filled with sand and rocks.

When we paddled back toward the blind, I could see what looked like a very tall man standing in the reeds. My heart froze. My stomach tightened.

"Dad," I said. "Who is that?"

I watched my dad squint toward the blind where we had just been sitting a few minutes earlier.

"Shit," he said. "I think that's the game warden."

I didn't know what that was or meant, but I had a sense that we were in trouble.

"He's gonna bust us for shooting past our limit," he said.

"What should we do?"

"Just keep paddling, babe. I'll talk to him." For some reason I couldn't understand, my dad was smiling when he said this. After all the trouble he had been in with various forms of the law, I couldn't fathom why this would be amusing to him.

But when we got to the blind, I was surprised that the figure was standing so still; it was like a statue. Then, all of a sudden, I got why my dad had been smiling. The figure I had seen was no person, but instead was my dad's thick hunting coat hanging from one of the reeds. He got a good kick out of seeing my gullibility. I think he was disappointed, though, that neither my brother nor I really got much out of the hunting trip. He had wanted it to be so much better, I think, but the fact was that we would rather have been at home playing our Nintendo than being out in the cold, shooting ducks.

The worst part was when we got back to the camp and he made us clean and gut all of the ducks we had killed. He showed us how to do the first one, then left us under the camp where the porch rose out over the water to do the rest. At first the feel of the warm guts and blood on my hands was almost unbearable, but after the second or third duck I started to get used to it and developed a certain detachment from what I was doing. It even felt good to know I was being of use. After we finished and cleaned off our hands we spent the rest of the afternoon watching TV, our dad letting us sip from his orange and brown bottle of Drambuie—to warm us up, he said—and shooting skeet that my dad slung out over the canal from the raised back porch of the camp.

*

I've always appreciated that my dad took the time and made the effort, as sporadic as that may have been, to bond with my brother and me. His attempts may have been failures, like the time he took us all to Grand Isle—an old resort town in the southernmost portion of Louisiana, now defunct, mostly— unaware that the International Tarpon Rodeo was going on at the time. This is, to my knowledge, the oldest fishing tournament in the United States, and people come from all over to participate in it, filling up the ramshackle hotels and motels all the way up Highway 1. As a result, after a nearly three-hour drive, we learned that there was nowhere to stay and had to settle for a room about an hour outside of Grand Isle which was infested with fleas, had no air conditioning, and was generally a shitty place.

The next day we had some better luck and got a small room in a motel in Grand Isle, but the place barely had running water—a thin pencil-line stream trickled from the bathtub faucet—was filled with an almost-suffocating moldy smell, and there were not enough beds for our family since my mom and sister had come along on this particular trip. My brother and I ended up sleeping on the floor. I wonder if my dad felt like a failure because of trips like this. As a father of my own two children now, I know the feeling of letting your family down, or at least of feeling as though you have. But I can say that I think back on these times fondly, that I appreciate my dad for making an effort, for trying to bring us all together.

One night while we were in Grand Isle, he took us all "gigging" for flounder in the shallows of the brown beach. What you do is hold a lantern and walk just to the point where the sand meets the water and when you see the shape of a flat fish move under the sand, you take a spear and stab the fish as fast as you can. My brother and I took turns holding the lantern and the spear and my dad egged us on as we walked farther and farther away from where my mom and my sister sat next to the bonfire we had built in the sand. They had become a small orange speck against the night sky. We didn't gig a single fish.

The next morning, despite tropical storm-force winds pummeling us on the beach, my dad used a Coleman burner to make gritty pancakes and eggs for us. By this point, I think he realized how badly the trip was going and so he refused to hear our complaints about breakfast, making us each eat at least two pancakes, which were all thick with brown sand from the beach. I can still remember the sand gritting in my teeth as I chewed. But now all these years later, I think this is a good memory to have. It's real. Both good and bad.

9.

I still had the cast on my arm when I went to a friend's house the next weekend for a campout. He had invited me, along with a few other boys from school, to come over to where he lived in a trailer in the woods in Folsom, not too far from where I lived. It was cold outside, expected to dip into the teens that night, but my friend's parents had a small shed in the backyard where we planned to sleep if it got too cold. There were some portable heaters back in there, and we figured we'd be all right.

My friend was actually a foster child, so these weren't his real parents, and they also had three other kids living in the house too, all of them fostered. The parents told us as soon as we got there that we were not allowed inside of the trailer for any reason whatsoever. We were to stay outside until the next morning when our parents came to pick us up. None of us thought this would be a problem. There were probably about ten of us all told, and as dusk came down, we wandered the woods and went into an abandoned house, breaking a few windows and then running off into one of the cowfields that lined the road. As it got darker we started to make our way back to my friend's house so that we could build a fire.

None of us had any type of camping equipment or proper clothes for sleeping outside in below-freezing temperatures. I don't think we told our parents that we had planned to sleep outside, and if we had, I don't suppose they imagined we would stick with the plan. They also probably assumed that the parents would relent and let us all come in. They didn't. We stood in the backyard and made a small bonfire in front of the toolshed where we planned to sleep that night. The shed was made out of tin with a wooden door padlocked shut on the front. My friend's parents must've at least given him the key or unlocked the door before we got there, because we didn't have to ask them to let us in the shed.

The floor inside was cement and covered with oil stains and dirt. There was a single window with cracked glass that looked out over the dark pasture and the thick woods beyond that. You could already see a thin skein of ice forming on the window, as the air in Louisiana is always damp and in the cold, the water turns quickly to ice. The shed was lined with plywood countertops covered with dangerous tools and boxes of roofing nails that spilled out onto the cold concrete floor where we were going to sleep. One of the kids there, Fred Wichers, stepped on one of the rusty nails and it went right through his tennis shoe and into his foot. We all sat out in front of the fire and tried to calm him down after we pulled out the nail. We were all too scared to go inside and ask to use the telephone to call his parents.

As the fire died down and we ran out of sticks and pine needles to throw on top of it, we all started to retreat into the shed. While the uninsulated walls did little to keep out the cold, there were two small space heaters on the counters and a single lightbulb dangling from one of the overhead rafters that made it feel a little bit warmer than it was outside. We fidgeted around and tried to think of something to do. Imagine ten boys, all around the age of eleven, trapped in a fifteen-by-twenty foot shed. Imagine that shed full of rusty tools and cobwebs, no radio, no television, the temperature—even with our combined body heat—probably about twenty degrees. And imagine that there is nothing to do for the next eight hours until when the sun comes up and their parents come down the gravel drive to pick them all up. That was us. We were bored. It was palpable. The novelty of this campout had quickly worn off and we wanted to be in our beds, under our blankets, in the heat of our houses.

My friend's foster brother, Billy, was probably the most restless of all of us. He had already tried to sneak into his parents' trailer a couple of times and had been chased out by his broom-wielding foster mother. When he told her that he just had to go to the bathroom and he didn't have any toilet paper, she told him to use a handful of leaves. And so he did this, sitting behind a rotten tree stump and laughing as we all watched the lethargic black shapes of cows inching toward him curiously. Billy was also the one who had broken the windows in that abandoned house we had come across earlier, running over the deadfall toward us and screaming that an old man was in the house and he was coming after us. It wasn't until way later when we were in the shelter of a stand of pines that he said he was just messing around with us, that the house was empty and dark. When we wanted to go back, he said it probably wasn't a good idea.

Billy was the oldest of us. He was thirteen but he was still in the same grade. He had been suspended from school multiple times and had been held back as a result. We all looked up to him, and we also were scared of him. He wasn't a mean kid, but there was a wild streak about him that made us believe he would do anything, absolutely *anything*, without thinking about the consequences. At some point in the evening, before it got dark, he had sneaked into his bedroom by climbing through the window and had hidden in one of the bunk beds. When his foster mom heard a noise back there in the room and had discovered him she beat him over the head with her hands, running behind him as he ran out of the house and jumped down from the back door onto the hard ground. There was no porch leading away from the trailer, just a couple of cinder block steps going up to the back door, and even those were crooked and not held down by anything, making the whole endeavor of going inside or outside the trailer a pretty dangerous affair.

Billy had also taken some of his foster mom's *Playgirl* magazines from her bathroom. He took them out to the shed and passed them around to us as we all laughed at the male models inside, but probably all secretly compared our undeveloped, prepubescent selves to the unrealistic images before us. After we tired of those, which didn't take long, I think Billy threw the magazines out in the woods somewhere. I never did see them after that.

Anyway, we were all in the tool shed, standing around one of the portable heaters and rubbing our hands together to keep them warm. Fred, the boy who had stepped on the roofing nail, was still sobbing in the corner, but we had started to forget about him by now, our minds already collectively racing toward what trouble we could stir up. The tension was almost palpable and it made me nervous. I wasn't the youngest, or the weakest, and since Fred was injured, he drew the most attention, just not the positive kind. We were almost like a pack of wild dogs or lions, the lame animal being the one targeted for killing or abuse. You could feel the eyes of the other boys looking at him, thinking up a way to shut him up.

Just then, Billy came up from underneath one of the plywood counters with a cardboard box. Its corners were soggy with oil or grease and strands of thick spider webs came off of it as he pulled it out of the dark hole where it had been sitting for God knows how long. He placed the box on the countertop and started pulling out its contents: cans of WD40, socket wrenches, small engine oil, lawnmower manuals, and then two dirty boxing gloves. The gloves were torn in places and you could see right through them where the stitching had come loose. They looked more like toys than real boxing gloves; they were much too small for any of us. Billy tried to pull them over his hands. They barely came down to his wrists but he was still able to make a fist and punch with them.

We watched him shadow box the air for a while, the overhead light above him casting his lithe shadow over the corrugated walls of the shed as he bobbed and weaved and punched at the air. Then he stopped and, still breathing heavily, asked if we wanted to fight.

Somebody pointed out the fact that we had only one pair of gloves.

"So what," Billy said. "We can each wear one."

He started to take off one of the gloves and tried to pass it to one of us. We were all reluctant to take it. Not only was he older and bigger than us, but we had all seen him fight. He was quick, brutal, and he was all heart. Even though we may not have understood that intellectually then, we knew on some visceral level that that was the most dangerous kind of fighter. Like my dad.

"Come on," Billy said. "Somebody spar with me."

Billy seemed light, almost playful, as he usually was. Despite the trouble he got in, he really was a sweet kid. I didn't make eye contact with him, though, because I didn't want to even play-fight with him. Even though my dad had shown me how to box here and there—he had been a Golden Gloves champion when he was a teenager, and he really knew how to fight—I was still afraid of Billy. Somebody else finally took the glove from him, though, and they soon were circling each other in the cramped shed like two roosters about to tear into each other.

The rest of us watched them and then finally they started throwing punches. Billy was fast. He dodged and weaved and swung in a fluid motion that was almost hypnotizing to watch. There was something almost painful about the expression on his face—it was as though he were fighting some image in his head rather than the boy in front of him. Billy looked at once sad and angry, and this is what made him so terrifying to me. That he could completely lose himself in an endeavor like this. You didn't know what was going to happen.

The match ended though, both boys walking to opposite sides of the shed to catch their breath and pass their gloves on to someone else. This went on a few more times, me casually avoiding the glove until Billy finally pointed out that it was only me and one other boy, Chris Meyers, who hadn't fought yet. Chris was a good friend of mine from school, and he was tall and very skinny. But since he was taller than I was, his arms were longer and he had a much better reach. I didn't want to fight him.

"Come on," Billy said. "Don't be such a pussy."

Chris was already putting his one glove on and dancing around the room like a real boxer and everyone else was looking at me, waiting.

"I can't," I said, pointing out the short cast on my right hand. "I have this." Since my dad had hacked more than half of it off, it was hardly a nuisance, hardly noticeable, and I think that my bone had started to mostly heal by then anyway, so no one had really even paid much attention to the cast until now.

"So what," Billy said. "You only have to use your left hand anyway."

He was right. But I just didn't like to fight. Now I would have to. I put the glove on and walked into the center of the shed and held up my arm to guard my face. Billy put his hand over both Chris's and my gloves and pushed them down like a referee in a real boxing match and then he asked if we were ready. We both nodded and Billy let go of our gloves and we started swinging. My instinct was to pull my leg up and back up toward the wall, bending myself as low as I could get so that Chris's gloved fist just landed on the top of my skull instead of hitting me in the face.

When I was completely cornered, someone backed Chris off of me and then we had more room to swing again. I finally swung a couple of times but Chris's arms were just too long and he was able to keep distance enough so that none of my punches landed, or when they did, they didn't do much damage. He swung a few more times, the cold glove stinging the sides of my face as he hit me and then I just went down. I wasn't really hurt but I didn't want to do this anymore. The other boys sort of booed at me and my quick end to the fight. I was embarrassed. I felt like a coward. Billy came over to me and asked if I was all right, though, and he told the other kids to be quiet, that it was not fair since I had a bum arm. He patted me on the back and stood me up, then quickly changed everyone's focus to something else.

The cold became nearly unbearable as the night wore on. We could all see our breath in front of us, despite the space heaters, and outside it looked as though sleet were starting to come down. We were all tired, and my head was starting to hurt from the cold, the exhaustion, and from being whacked in the face. It felt as though someone were continually punching me in the eye and I could feel the blood pulsing. The light made it worse. The sounds inside the shed made it worse. Nothing I did helped so I just sat down and closed my eyes as tightly as I could and I rubbed at my aching temples with my fingers.

The pain didn't go away. Eventually, it got so bad that I became nauseated. The nausea increased until I finally stood up and pushed out the door and threw up next to the smoldering pile of sticks and boxes that had been our bonfire earlier. I had an immediate sense of relief. It was as though someone had pulled a stopper out of my ear and let out all the pressure from my head. Now I was just exhausted. I had to get some sleep.

I went back in the shed and some of the other boys were moving things around, trying to make a pallet for us to lie down on. They were tearing up boxes and smoothing out the greasy cardboard over the concrete. They used their shoes to brush aside nails and dirt and they took their jackets and rolled them up into pillows. Billy stood on a milk crate and we helped him pull down a giant, Queen-sized box spring from between a couple of the rafters overhead. The box spring had been eaten away by mice or rats and you could see inside the holes in the fabric where wasps had made nests, long deserted now, and where the mice or rats that had gnawed away at the fabric had made nests as well. It was full of pine needles and hay, all bunched up and strung together with cobwebs or strands of fabric and string. The wood frame of the box spring had splotches of black mold on it, surrounded by crooked white circles of mildew so that it looked as if someone had cracked a small egg with black yolk on the little pieces of wood holding the thing together.

Then all of us lay down next to each other and Billy put the box spring on top of us. He pulled the string to kill the lightbulb overhead and climbed under the box spring too and we tried to sleep like that. Time ticked away very slowly as the cold continued to creep in, getting under our flesh and making our bones hurt. I must've eventually fallen asleep, but I don't think I slept long.

The next morning, when we went outside, it was still early and the sky was gray and cold. Everything felt damp and the sticks where our little fire had been were charred and black and smoldering still. None of us tried to relight it. My friend's foster parents were up—we could see the kitchen light on—but they still wouldn't let us inside the trailer so we all stood out in the cold and waited for our parents to pick us up.

A couple of days later, my dad took me to the orthopedist to get the rest of my cast removed and the doctor was stunned by what my dad had done. He told my dad what a serious injustice he had done to me by cutting off most of the cast like that, that my arm would never heal properly and that I would suffer the rest of my life now, thanks to him. Maybe the doctor was being dramatic, but my dad looked embarrassed being scolded like that in front of me. Usually he was the one in control and usually he fought back, but this time he just sat there and listened as the doctor sucked his teeth and shook his head in disbelief as he used his little buzzing saw to cut the cast off of my arm.

Part Two
1990s

10.

I woke up one night to the sound of my mom calling out for help. Then I heard her screaming, followed by a loud thump. My brother and I both got out of our beds and opened the door to our room, looked down the dark hallway where we could see my dad choking my mom and pounding her head against the front door. She was holding the portable phone in her hand and as I ran over to her, she tossed the phone to me and told me with what breath she had left to call 911. I held the phone and dialed, but before I could talk to anyone, my dad took the phone from my hand and threw it at the wall. It broke into about twenty pieces.

By this point my brother was trying to pull my dad from off of my mom, and since my dad was focused on yelling at me now for calling the police, my brother was able to pull him away. My mom slouched down to the floor and put her hands around her neck, which was red from my dad's thick hands.

"Go to bed," my dad told us. "This is none of y'all's business."

We didn't answer him, but went over to my mom to see if she was all right. My dad stepped away from us, breathing hard and taking in the scene which he had created. He had a look of disbelief on his face, mixed with anger and a sort of drunken confusion. He sat down on the sofa and lit a cigarette.

"She hit me first," he said, as though we had asked him to try to justify what he had been doing. My dad had always taught us never to hit a woman—not for any reason—and here he was almost choking my mom to death. We ignored him.

My mom was still sitting on the floor next to the front door and I was trying to gather the pieces of the phone. After a few minutes we could see the blue lights from the police cars coming through the dark and up the long driveway toward our trailer. Apparently my call had gone through and even though I hadn't said anything over the phone, the dispatcher had sent someone out anyway.

My dad started cursing me, telling me he wasn't going to hurt anyone. He was just defending himself. Now the police were involved. He told us to stay the fuck out of it.

The cops came up to the porch and we could hear their boots clomping on the boards and their radios going off on their belts as they approached. I stood up and turned on the porchlight and then opened the front door before they knocked.

But the police didn't arrest my dad that night. They told him to go inside and stay there until he sobered up. They told my mom that they could just as well take her to jail for hitting my dad first, which there was no proof of, and they told me and my brother to stay out of our parents' business. We had no place getting involved, they said.

When they pulled away about twenty minutes later, my brother and I went back to our room and I started packing a small duffel bag with some clothes. I was going to leave the next morning. My brother and I talked a little about what had happened, and after a while, we both got in our beds and tried to get some sleep before the alarm went off at 6:30 to wake us up for school. We were in the eleventh grade.

The next morning, when we came out of our room to leave for school, my mom was sitting on the sofa in the dark. You could tell she had been up all night. I could see their bedroom door was closed and I knew that my dad was in there, probably still sleeping.

"What are you doing with that bag?" my mom said.

"I'm not coming home after school today," I told her.

"David, don't do that," she said. "Why would you do that?"

"I can't live here anymore. Not like this."

"Well—" was all she said.

I drove with my brother to school that morning in the little Mazda pickup truck we shared and which used to be my dad's and I told my brother that he could take the truck home, that he would need it more since I could get rides with friends. I had a plan to stay with a couple of people I knew from school. That afternoon, when class let out, I got a ride to a friend's who was staying with his sister and brother-in-law in a trailer park in Abita Springs. In exchange for letting me stay there, I told them I would work hanging drywall for my friend's brother-in-law, who owned a small business and had about three or four other guys working for him.

We were about to have some time off of school for Christmas holidays and my plan was to stay there in the trailer park, work and save up some money, then go somewhere else from there. Every morning we would wake up at about 4:30 to go to work. We would drive out with Charles, my friend's brother-in-law, in his little truck to some house in the country and he would buy us breakfast at Burger King or McDonald's and we would eat and try to wake ourselves up as the sky went from black to a heavy gray. The sun never seemed to come out on those days, and it was always cold and rainy outside.

Charles was a nice guy, though. He was about ten years older than I was, he had a little boy to whom he was a good dad. He took me in and let me live with him, treated me like a friend, a peer even, told me jokes and stories, showed me how to hang drywall, and let me party with him and his other friends every evening after work.

When we pulled up at the trailer park in the late afternoon, there were already a few cars parked in the spaces leading up to his trailer. We got out of the truck, tired from hard physical work all day, and went inside where someone immediately poured us strong drinks. You could tell that some of them were already drunk and they wanted us to catch up. A guy named Aaron who also worked with Charles sometimes, poured me a tall screwdriver and everyone stood in the kitchen and pounded on the counter, encouraging me to down the whole drink as fast as I could. When the glass was empty, someone poured me another one. Then another. After only about fifteen minutes, I walked out of the kitchen, then out to the lot in front of the trailer to piss. Everything was spinning. I had been drunk plenty of times before but this was different. I was hallucinating.

I stood in the dark behind someone's car and pissed in the yard, then I heard someone walking up behind me. It was Charles's younger brother, Waylon. He was probably about two or three years older than me. He offered me a cigarette and another screwdriver and we walked around the trailer park and talked, eventually ending up in a gazebo that was at the entrance to the park. When we got back to the trailer, someone had some pot and so we smoked that and watched TV until we fell asleep. I was enjoying the freedom of not living with my parents and being able to do whatever I wanted to do.

The next morning Charles came into the den and woke us up at 4:30. It was time to go to work again.

I did this every day for a couple of weeks. We worked, we went home and got drunk, high, sometimes the neighbors would be over and would get into fights, which we all got involved in, trying to break them up. Then we would do the same thing again the next day. And the day after that.

At some point, my dad found out where I was living and he pulled up one night with my mom in the passenger seat of the van and he started to throw garbage bags that were filled with my clothes and other belongings out into the wet yard. My mom just sat there quietly as he unloaded the back of the van, then they left. Some people helped me take my stuff inside and we threw it in a corner and smoked some more pot and drank some more alcohol.

One night I sat on the sofa and nursed an entire bottle of Old Crow all by myself. I was smoking Camel cigarettes and just taking little sips in between conversations and playing music, so it didn't occur to me how much I'd had to drink until I stood up and realized that I could barely stand. I fell back onto the sofa and everyone laughed at me. Not in a mean way, but more of a way that suggested they were proud of me, that we were all on the same team. It felt good to belong to a family like this, to be accepted, to feel liked.

I made a point to hold up the empty bottle and drop my cigarette into it before I finally managed to push myself off of the sofa and across the small den so that I could go out to the porch and piss. I ended up puking off the side of the porch instead. And once I got started I couldn't stop. I threw up more than what could have possibly been inside of me. I hobbled off the porch and went into the grass and lay down, lifting my head every now and then to throw up even more.

My stomach started to cramp, my throat burned, and when there was nothing left to throw up, I puked up snot, then after that, I dry heaved. I was sick for three days, unable to eat or even move. Eventually, not being able to work, I had to move back home with my mom and dad.

*

When I was fifteen I wrote my biological mother a letter. I referred to her as "Susie," despite her later wish that I call her "Susan"—not "Mom," but the more romanticized, and inappropriate, I thought, "Susan." The thought of her was something that had never quite left me. I would steal pictures of her from my grandmother's dry sink, an old wooden sink where she kept large containers and shoe boxes full of family photos. I kept an old black-and-white picture of her from when she was in high school in my wallet—next to pictures of girls I was dating. I had a picture of her at Fort Walton Beach in Florida, her eyes squinting against the sun, her hair blowing in the wind. My mother used to be quite beautiful before her illness ravaged her—now her teeth are orange and rotting, she is filthy and malodorous, with wide, wild eyes.

I didn't know how to feel about her then. I didn't blame her for leaving me. I was happy enough in my life and had been told countless times how ill my mother was, how incapable of raising me she was, how much better off I was without her. I believed that, and I still know it to be true. But I would stare at those old pictures of her and wonder about who she was—fantasize about meeting her. I was infinitely curious about her. Not long after I wrote the letter to her, Bobby, her husband since not long after she gave me up, or since I was taken from her, as she remembers it, called me at our trailer in Folsom.

I talked on the phone with him for several hours. He was a very intelligent, kind person. He answered all of my questions about my mother, told me how she was doing, said that she had read my letter, but that he didn't think it was a good idea for us to speak just yet. He warned me of how my mother might react to me. He said she might treat me more like a boyfriend than a son, that she was incapable of making that distinction. He said that she would probably want to hold my hand and generally just act inappropriately toward me. He said that he would have her write me back. I never did get a letter. Years later, I would learn from my mother that my grandmother, who now lived on the other side of the property in Folsom where we lived, would intercept any letter or card that Susie sent to me, and it was another five years before I finally met my biological mother in person.

11.

It had been months leading up to my dad finally being fired from his job—coming in late, drinking during his lunch hour, provoking fights with the other employees. When he came home after his last day at work, he was in an almost incomprehensible state of rage. Yet he calmly walked into the house, changed his clothes, used the bathroom, then went into his closet and grabbed one of his shotguns and loaded it. My mom and younger sister were outside feeding the animals and they could hear him coming around the trailer before they saw him.

"*Gretch?*" he called out, calmly, almost sweetly.

She didn't answer. Something about his tone alarmed her, so she stayed near the chicken coop with my then seven-year-old sister, waiting to see what my dad's intent was. She hadn't known yet that he had been fired, but his behavior by this point had grown so unpredictable and erratic she thought it best to wait and see what he was up to.

He continued around the side of the trailer, past the little garden and the tall fig tree that grew next to it, temporarily putting him out of sight. He called out again and as he came into view, my mom saw the gun in his hands, its black barrel pointing out toward her and my sister.

My mom grabbed my sister's hand and started running. Pure instinct kicked in. They ran from the chicken coops behind the green shed and over the muddy backyard, crossing the horse paddocks and the clay mound where a barn was supposed to have been built, but never was. My little sister's tiny legs and feet struggled to keep up as they ran, my dad now walking patiently behind them with the shotgun. Not running, just keeping a steady pace, the gun held out before him, still calling calmly for his wife and daughter to come see.

When they got to my grandparents' house across the property, they ran inside and locked the door behind them. My mom grabbed the phone and called the police as my dad slowly came up the driveway and onto the porch. He was still unusually calm as he knocked on the door. They told him to go away, that they had already called the police. They said they didn't know what he was doing, but that he was scaring them. To everyone's surprise, he turned around and walked back across the property with his shotgun, and then he holed himself up in the trailer and called my mom at my grandmother's house.

He told her that if the police were coming that he was not

going to surrender. They would have to come into the trailer and get him. They would have to kill him, he said, before he came outside. Before long, a stream of police cruisers was making its way down the hill at the foot of the property and snaking over the gravel driveway, their lights blinking as they made their way to the trailer—they had been there many times before so there was no confusion about which side of the property to go to.

They lined up in the driveway and the police started to fill the yard, their weapons drawn, having been informed by my mom that my dad was inside the trailer with a gun and that he had said he would not come out. They called to him on their megaphone, gave him one chance to come out. Then they waited. After a few minutes the SWAT team arrived and they went around to the backyard in their black uniforms and Kevlar jackets and staked out a position. Now they could see my dad through the large kitchen windows.

There was a standoff, but it didn't last hours like you see on TV. After some tense minutes my dad came out of the trailer and surrendered. They threw him down and handcuffed him, then put him in the back of one of their cruisers and took him away.

I was at work when I got the phone call telling me what had happened. I was not surprised or shocked by the news, and it actually came as sort of a relief, as I knew that my dad being in jail would ease some of the tensions at home.

This time my mom said that when he was released from jail on bond he could not come back home. He would have to live with his mother in Chalmette. So that is where he went when he got out of jail. He got another job with a local union, working as an electrician again, started attending AA meetings, and began the process of getting my mom to take him back. It didn't take him long either. His promises to stop drinking, to be home more, to work, stay out of trouble—it was the same thing we had all been hearing for years, but he was able to convince my mom that this time he really meant it. This time he was really going to change.

So I wasn't terribly surprised when I got home from work one night and saw my dad's cigarettes on the kitchen counter in their usual spot, his wallet on top of the refrigerator where he had always kept it. At first I thought that maybe my mom had accidentally brought some of his things home after visiting him in Chalmette, that maybe he left them in her van and she just brought them inside out of habit, but then I went into the laundry room to get a snack and could hear my dad snoring in the bedroom that he shared with my mom.

I was furious. I couldn't understand how he could be out of jail so quickly, let alone how my mom could let him in the house after what he had done. My brother came home a few minutes later from his job and I told him that Dad was home again. He looked surprised too, but didn't seem to be angered by it like I was. We sat in the den and watched TV like we usually did after getting home late from work, often staying awake until three or four in the morning.

At some point my dad woke up and came into the kitchen for a cigarette. He often woke up two or three times in the middle of the night to smoke, and this time he told us that he wanted to talk to us about some things. He told us to follow him back into the bedroom, where he lay down in the bed next to my mom, trying to look confident and in full control of the environment and of the situation.

"I know y'all don't want me here," he said. "But this is the way things are going to be. If you don't like it, you can leave."

I looked over at my mom, who didn't say anything. I knew right then that he had already talked her into being complicit with whatever plan he had in his head now. He was good at that—wearing you down with words like someone rubbing away at a piece of wood or a rock with a coarse sheet of sandpaper.

"I need y'all to be with me on this," he said. "If you're not with us, you're against us."

Us. I assumed he meant him and my mom. I couldn't believe what I was hearing. I felt betrayed, even though I knew the power of control he could have. Still, he had been gone. He had been locked up. Why the hell was he back again, lying in bed like he was the king of the castle and telling us how things were going to be again?

He tried to sound contrite.

"Look, I know I messed up. I'm going to quit drinking. I just need y'all to help."

My brother and I listened, but we didn't say anything.

"First you can't have any more contact with your grandparents. No one else in the family either. They're all against us and we have to stick together if this is going to work."

We watched him as he smoked one cigarette after another and told us what his plan was. We knew better than to dissent.

"I'm going to start going to AA meetings. I already have a sponsor. I want y'all to go too. Okay?"

No answer.

"Okay?" he said.

"Yeah," I said. My brother nodded his consent. I knew he was probably as mad, if not madder, than I was.

"I'm also going to start up a business. I want to start selling birds. I need y'all's help getting some cages put in the shed. That means y'all have to get all y'all's shit out of there. The punching bag, your bikes, anything else that'll be in the way."

"Okay."

"It's not going to be easy to do all this financially since I don't have a job right now."

He had been laid off already from his union job as an electrician.

"So I'm gonna need y'all's help paying the bills around here too. How much do y'all make at your jobs?"

I was working at a phone answering service and my brother was working in a restaurant. We each made about two hundred dollars a week. We told him.

"Well we're going to need that money. Each time you get paid, we're going to have to get your paychecks so that we can pay the bills and eat. Just until I get this business off the ground. Once I do, I promise I'll pay you back every cent."

In the past, my dad had been pretty good about paying us back any money he borrowed from us. Once he had come into our room on Christmas Day after everyone had gone home and asked—albeit with a little shame on his face—if he could borrow the money my brother and I had gotten for Christmas that day. We handed it over to him and he put it in his pocket and left. Two weeks later, though, he did pay us back. With interest.

My brother and I felt we had no choice but to agree to my dad's plan. We wanted to stay home and help my mom and younger sister and we knew that if we left, things would likely be a lot worse for them.

But things got worse anyway. My dad sincerely did try to stop drinking but his idea of success meant that every one of us would be involved as well. My mom went with him to AA meetings, attending the Al-Anon meetings down the hall. My dad was working as an electrician again, but only sporadically, so we still didn't have any money. My brother and I handed over our paychecks every other week, and we all struggled to survive.

True to his word, my dad started building a sort of aviary in the shed behind our trailer. He had been in contact with a woman who sold birds and other exotic animals and he started buying cockatiels from her to build up his stock and to begin breeding his own birds. It was slow going but he dove into this new project. He also started to bring home massive amounts of junk from the various jobs he was getting: old light fixtures, scores of milk crates filled with rusted wall sconces, long screws, nuts, bolts, wires. He stored all of this under the trailer by the back porch, where the rainwater would spill down and wet it all, a thick rust blanketing everything he brought home.

Eventually, he bought a trailer to hitch to the back of their green minivan, which he began to load with more tools and flea market finds that he would buy impulsively with what little money we had. He started to keep stacks of papers and notebooks and pens, calculating and devising and making lists. It was the strangest I had ever seen him act. And he got worse.

While he wasn't drinking anymore, he still smoked about two packs of cigarettes a day, and his smoker's cough was worse than it had ever been. He gasped for breath, and he moaned in pain as he coughed and hacked up mucous non-stop. A couple of times I went with him and my mom to sell birds on the side of the road: they would park the minivan in a gravel lot beside the highway and set up the cages full of cockatiels and hope someone would stop to buy some. At twenty-five dollars a bird, it was hard to make any money, so sometimes they would go to a flea market in Mississippi and rent a table. More often than not, they came back home with more stuff than they left with, my dad's impulse to buy things he didn't need but that he thought he could use "one day" growing along with his physical illness.

It was difficult to watch my dad deteriorate that way. Here was a man who was once so strong and virile that he had kicked the back window out of a police cruiser while he was in handcuffs after he'd been thrown back there after a fight he had gotten into. A man who everyone in jail called "Chief," despite his small stature—he was about five-foot-five—and who commanded a sort of fearful respect from everyone he encountered. His physical strength had once been frightening, and now you could just push him over with one hand. It is one of the saddest things to watch a man being eaten away by illness, all that he was and had been melting away like ice in a cup left out on a porch rail in the summer.

When he finally went to the doctor, he was diagnosed with pulmonary fibrosis. The doctors attributed this to the factories he had worked in as a teenager in Chalmette, to his exposure to asbestos in some of the old buildings he worked in, and of course, to his smoking. But he didn't give up the cigarettes. When it got so bad that he was on an oxygen machine, he would trail it behind him as he smoked, stopping every couple of steps to catch his breath or untangle himself from the plastic tube that went from the highly-combustible tank of air and to his nose, where it hissed out breath for him.

After one of his lungs collapsed, we had to take him to a charity hospital in Franklinton, where they transferred him to University Hospital in New Orleans after they said there was nothing they could do to help him. My mom stayed there with him for all of the days he was hospitalized, and the one time when I went to visit him, I was shocked by his appearance—his skin had turned a purplish-gray color—his entire body swollen, puffy. Some medical students filed into his room during my visit in order to poke at his chest and neck with their fingers—the doctors who were training them explained that they would probably never see anything like this again in their careers. What had happened, they said, was that the air from my dad's collapsed lung was leaking into the rest of his body, causing him to puff up like that. He looked like a blow-up version of himself.

My dad was a good sport about this, though, even about

the man lying next to him in the small, dingy room who moaned incessantly, calling out for his mother. But it was almost too much for me to bear. It was hard on my mom too. She stayed faithfully next to him in that dark room, sleeping on an uncomfortable cot and listening to him hack away his lungs night and day and cursing her and complaining that he needed a cigarette and that he was going to kill himself if he didn't get out of that place. Finally they let him go.

My dad was facing some serious jail time now as well—at least two years, the lawyers had told him. He had gotten his third DWI, was also charged with driving under a suspended license, carrying a concealed weapon, resisting arrest, being a public nuisance, and the list went on. At night, I would hear him sitting at the kitchen table, talking to himself and sometimes sobbing softly. Smoking one cigarette and lighting the next one before the first was even out.

The day he was supposed to report to the jail to start serving out his sentence was gray and rainy. He wanted us to drop him off "as a family." So my brother, my little sister, and I all climbed into the van and rode in silence as my mom drove my dad to the jail. When we pulled up, we got out of the car and my dad hugged me and my brother, told us to take care of my mom and sister and the house, then he hugged and kissed my little sister and my mom, who was crying, and we watched him walk through the automatic doors like they have at the entrance to the grocery store.

As with the other times when my dad was going to be gone for a while, there was a sense of relief that came over me. I felt guilty for feeling this way. It's not that I wanted him to be in jail, but it was just easier on all of us when he was gone. We didn't have to deal with his unpredictable outbursts of violence, his erratic behavior, his drinking. There was a tangible weight in the air when he was home, and so everyone usually just stayed in their rooms with the doors closed while he lay on the sofa in his robe and underwear, watching movie after movie and smoking one cigarette after the next.

They finally gave him a compassionate release from jail when it became clear that he was not going to live much longer. He was slow moving and his face was pulled taut with the pain he was in, though he never complained. Save for the oxygen tank he toted behind him, he didn't look ill. He never lost much weight, maintaining his stocky, fighter's build until the very end of his life. Sometimes I could hear him moaning on the sofa as he tried to hold back the coughing fits that, once started, could go on for half an hour. That is what pained him the most, I think. The coughing, which kept him from breathing, causing a pain in his chest that probably felt as if someone were stacking cinder blocks on top of him one after the other. I'm imagining this now. But he never really let on how much pain he was in, save for moaning occasionally and cursing under his breath after a really bad coughing jag.

He told my mom once that he was going to go in the backyard and out into the woods and just shoot himself because he was in so much pain. I think he had really made up his mind to do it, he had the gun and everything, but she talked him out of it by reminding him of how it would affect my little sister, who was not even nine years old yet.

The day before my dad died I was off work and ended up sitting next to him on the front porch while he lit up one cigarette after another and puffed lightly on them. He had usually inhaled his cigarettes very deeply but now it hurt so much to even breathe air that he could barely suck in any of the smoke. When he saw me looking at him, he looked kind of embarrassed, then took another small drag from his cigarette.

"I know it's stupid to be doing this, babe," he said. "But there's no point in quitting now."

He was sitting on the porch swing that we had chained to one of the rafters on the front porch and I was sitting on the stoop just by the screen door. He started asking me about my life, what I wanted to do with myself. He had never asked me anything like this, not even close to it, before. I told him that I still didn't know, that I was thinking about going back to college. I had dropped out after coming close to what I thought was a nervous breakdown and getting a pretty bad stomach ulcer as a result, when my dad started to get really bad with his drinking and then after he got fired and chased my mom and sister with a shotgun.

He said that I should definitely go back to school, get a degree. He told me how smart he had always thought I was, and that I shouldn't let that go to waste. I could do a lot with my life, he told me. I have to say that it was pretty surreal to hear him, my dad, tell me these things, to hear him speak so candidly and sincerely to me. There had been times when he showed emotion toward me, what felt like real love—the day my adoption was finalized, for example, I could see him holding back tears as he put his arm around me and held me close to him for a few seconds—but nothing he had said or done had ever come close to this before. Then he told me that he loved me. Even though I was kind of surprised by his saying this, I told him that I loved him too. And I'm glad I did, because it was the last time I ever saw him alive.

The next day, January 3, 2000, I was scheduled to go in to work at the bookstore where I had been working for the past few months after getting fired from the phone answering service I had worked at for almost a year. I had the afternoon shift, which meant I was supposed to go in at 4:30 and get off somewhere around 2 or 3 in the morning. Even though the store closed at 11, it was so mismanaged that it took a good three or four hours to close everything down and for the new managers to count out our tills and do their final paperwork. They wouldn't let us leave until they finished. A couple of times, I opened one of the VHS movies from the shelf and watched it in the kids' section of the store, where there was a little TV/VCR combo at the foot of a little wooden train. I would sit in the tiny train, my knees up to my chest, and watch movies until the overhead lights finally clicked off, letting me know it was time to leave.

Anyway, this particular day I was working at the register, feeling tired, trying to keep my eyes open—it was a Tuesday, so the store was nearly empty—when someone from the Customer Service desk called my name over the speaker to say I had a phone call. I closed my register, took off my apron, and walked to the middle of the store. Then I went up the platform to the Customer Service desk and picked up the black portable phone from where it was blinking in its cradle. It was hidden behind the large machine that we used to look up books back then.

It was my brother.

"Hey," he said.

"Hey, what's up?"

"Nothing, man. Dad had to go to the hospital again," he said.

"Shit, that sucks. What happened?"

"I don't know," he said. "But you might want to get over there. It seems pretty bad."

"What happened?" I asked him again.

He didn't want to tell me, I could tell, but I also could tell that something was really wrong this time.

"All right," I told him. "I'll get over there."

I hung up the phone and went to the storeroom in the back to look for one of the managers. When I found her in the back office after walking through a maze of boxes and shipping crates full of books, the dust in the false light back there like a scrim of gauze dripping from the stained-tile ceiling, I tried to sound nonchalant when I told her I had to leave early, that my dad was in the hospital. I honestly wasn't that upset, as I wasn't even sure what exactly was wrong with him. I expected it to be another false alarm. He would often get tangled up in the clear plastic tubes of his oxygen tank while sleeping, then he'd wake up in a panic when he couldn't breathe and couldn't get the tubes in his nose since they were all wrapped up around his body and the sheets on the bed.

The manager was listening to me while one of the other managers, Derlene, smirked and turned toward the time clock on the wall, as though what I was saying was somehow funny, or that she thought I was lying so that I could leave work early. I know I could give off the impression of being a slacker at that job, but come on, who would make up something like this just to go out and get drunk or go home and go to sleep? Maybe some people would, but not me. The manager told me she was sorry for my troubles and told me to come back to work after I saw my dad, if I could. She was short-staffed and needed my help closing up, she said. I told her I would, not even considering that as an option, even if my dad turned out to be all right. Like hell I was going to come back here to sweep up this place and clean the bathrooms. When I got a job at a bookstore, I had thought it would be more like working in a library—quiet and peaceful, surrounded by books and people who loved books. Instead I got paid $5.13 an hour to get yelled at by customers who wanted Pokémon cards for their kids or who were mad that we ran out of one of those god-awful *Left Behind* books. I was amazed by how much crap people consumed instead of reading real books. The only literature I think I ever sold there was to some bored-looking high school kids who had to read something for their English class. It was sad.

Anyway, I walked out of the stock room and went outside to the empty parking lot where my silver Ford Taurus was parked. It was quiet in the shopping center and it seemed as though no one was out at all. I got in my car and turned on the radio and started heading toward the highway. It was eerily un-crowded as I got on the ramp to the interstate, and I remember the Red Hot Chili Peppers' song "Breaking the Girl" was playing on the radio. I turned it up as loud as I could without busting my speakers and drove to the hospital.

When I pulled up, I parked and went into the Emergency Room where my brother had told me my dad would be. I asked about him at the desk and one of the nurses pointed me toward one of the triage rooms where my dad was. At this point I was still just thinking he had had an episode again with his breathing and that I would find him in the room in bed, the hiss of the oxygen tank restoring him back to some semblance of health. However, when I got to the triage and just before I started to pull back the blue curtain to go inside, a doctor walked out and took my shoulder.

The doctor told me that he wanted me to know that he had done everything he could to help, but that my dad was just too far gone by the time he had arrived. What this man was telling me hadn't registered yet. I didn't understand that he was telling me that my dad—the man who had raised me since I was two years old, the man with whom I had just spent half of the previous day talking to on the front porch, the man whom I had once watched help birth a baby colt on a cold winter morning, pulling the steaming horse from its mother and sitting in the hay and in the cold mud of the stall as we all watched the baby horse break out of its amniotic sac with its wet spindly legs, finally standing up and wobbling toward its mother, who nudged its wet coat as it looked for the place to nurse her—was dead. That had been on Martin

Luther King Day, I remember, and so we were off from school and it was unseasonably cold for Louisiana—probably in the twenties—and we could see our breath in front of our faces as we all sat there in the stall, which was warm from the light hanging from an orange extension cord overhead and from each of our bodies in the small space, watching my dad help bring a new life into this world. My sister named the horse Freedom. Months later, one of the other horses we kept in the paddock would kick my dad onto the hard, dusty ground and then stomp his chest, making a black bruise the size of a Frisbee that stayed there for weeks, like a tattoo. But my dad never went to the doctor for it, never punished the horse for kicking him either.

And now here was this doctor trying to tell me some bad news about the dad I remember taking us to a Mardi Gras parade and coming across a group of teenagers surrounding a younger boy next to a Dumpster behind a supermarket. They were taunting him. What got me was that there were lots of onlookers—families, adults, grown men, but no one did anything to help the little boy. When we passed the group of bullies, my dad waded in and broke it up and chased the bullies off, cursing after them as they ran. Still no one did anything, but the little boy looked grateful as he ran back toward the front of the store. That was the kind of man he was. He wasn't self-righteous or anything. He just did the right thing in situations like that. And even though he made his share of mistakes, here was this doctor telling me something that sounded like he was trying to say my dad was dead. That is what he told me. My dad was dead. He was sorry. Then he walked off to deal with the living again.

I pulled back the curtain and I walked inside the small room. My mom was sitting on a little chair next to a table and she was thumbing absent-mindedly through a phone book. I could tell she wasn't really seeing what was on the pages, she was just flipping through them. I looked over to where my dead father lay on the hospital bed, his skin a dark purple color and splotchy. His eyes were half shut and you could see just a slit of white, but no iris, no pupil, just white. He didn't have a shirt on and I kept looking at his chest, waiting for it to rise and fall, and for a moment, it looked as though it actually was moving, slowly ascending and descending as he took in breath, but I knew when I put my hand there and felt how cold, how stiff he was, that he was gone.

I couldn't cry. I wanted to, but the tears would not come. I hugged my mom and then the doctor came in again and reminded us that we needed to call a funeral home to come and collect the body. They always spoke this way about people who had died, using words like "collect." I then realized why my mom had been fingering the phone book when I first walked in, so I sat down and we called a place nearby. While we were waiting for the funeral home director to arrive, another doctor came into the room with a wooden clipboard. She placed the clipboard on my dad's dead chest and started taking notes. She asked us a few questions, poked at my dad's skin, saw one of the tattoos on his arm, then sucked her teeth as if she were judging him. She knew how he died. She seemed angry at having to be there. Well, we were too.

I walked my mom out of the hospital into the dark parking lot and we got into my car. I asked her where my brother was and she told me he had gone out to clear his head. He was the one who had found my dad, had to give him CPR while he waited for the ambulance to arrive, and he was very upset. She didn't know where he was.

We were quiet as we drove back up the long stretch of Highway 25 toward Folsom. The tall pines were blurred in the windshield and under the glare of the headlights of my Ford Taurus, and the cars coming by on the other side of the road were like mirages somehow, as if none of this was real.

My mom told me how earlier that day my dad had asked her if the holidays were over. She told him that, yes, it was January 3, and all the holidays were done. Good, he had told her. That's good. A little while later when she told him she was going to the store with my little sister, he told her to take her time, that he'd be all right. Now my mom was saying that it was as though my dad was planning to die today, that he had held out until the holidays were over, and that now he was ready to surrender. Like I've said, he was the kind of man who could bowl you over with these unexpected moments of sensitivity and compassion. He could be such a hardass one minute then do or say something like that that would bring you to tears the next.

Just to give you another example of this, I'll tell you real quick about when I was in the eighth grade and one of my classmates brought a gun to school. We were sitting in the gym at morning assembly and listening to one of the teachers call out from the list of students who had lunch detention or assignment hall. When he called this particular kid's name—Keith LaFrance—the kid stood up from where he was sitting in the bleachers and walked toward the center of the gym floor where the teacher, Mr. Hubbel, was standing. The kid was holding a small handgun and pointing it at the teacher, who stood stock-still in the center of the gym. No one moved.

When Mr. Hubbel broke the silence by trying to get Keith to put the gun down, some of the girls in the gym started to scream. As soon as that happened, kids started to get up. You could hear them running down the wooden bleachers, then you could hear the doors at the side of the gymnasium open as the kids started to run outside. The teachers steered the kids through the double-doors, trying to maintain a sense of order, and I could see that Keith was still standing in the center of the gym floor with his gun pointed at Mr. Hubbel.

I didn't run. A couple of friends and I stood up on the bleachers where we had been sitting and we watched the other kids tripping over one another as they tried to get out of the gym. We watched as the boy with the gun tried to corral some of the students into one spot, but he was unsuccessful. Then he pointed the gun directly at us and we just stood there and looked at him. Then he ran out of one of the back doors of the gym.

Once he was gone, one of the teachers told us to go to one of the empty classrooms and to not come out until they told us to. We casually walked to the back of the herd of other kids and waited for them to clear so we could get in the main hallway where the empty classrooms were quickly filling up. Once we were inside of the hall, one of the teachers ran a chain and padlock that had been on the outside of the doors through the handles on the inside of the door and then they locked the padlock shut and pushed us into one of the classrooms.

All of the kids were on the floor, hiding under the desks, crying, hugging one another, and the teachers just stood with blank faces at the front of the classroom, not knowing what to say or do. At some point, I was on the floor and crawled over to the window at the back of the classroom, where I had to stand up to look outside. As soon as I stood, I looked out of the window and could see the boy with the gun running across the field behind the classroom. I saw him stop at several of the windows and look inside. Within seconds he was at the window where I was standing and looking out. He pointed the gun directly at my face and I could see straight down the barrel. I could hear the sound of the metal tap against the glass as he pointed the gun at me. I looked at his eyes and at his face. His eyes darted from one side to the other as he held the gun on me, as though he were looking for someone else.

I waited for him to shoot me. I didn't want him to, understand, but I also was not afraid at that moment of being killed. As time unfurled slowly around me and I took in all of the details of the boy's face, the field behind him, the streaks and prints on the glass window, the rusted latch that you really had to put your weight on to get the window open, I felt a girl's hand grab my arm and pull me down to the floor. By the time I stood back up, the boy had run off. We heard several gun shots a few minutes later.

But he didn't kill anyone, that boy, hadn't even hit anyone either. He was arrested and our parents were called to come get us, the line of police cars and the cars of our parents already starting to pile up on the narrow road that led to our school. I was, for some reason, unfazed by any of this. I don't know if it's because I was too young to appreciate the gravity of what had happened or not, but I'll never forget that night when my dad came home from work and I passed him sitting on the sofa on my way to the kitchen. He was watching TV and the den was dark save for the blue light coming off the television set and illuminating me as I walked passed him.

"Your mom told me what happened at school today," he said.

"Yeah." I smiled a half smile (I got this from my mother).

"It's not funny, babe. You could've died, you know?"

"Yeah," I said.

"Well I'm glad you're all right."

I started to walk back into the kitchen but I looked at my dad, and to this day, I could swear I saw something damp just underneath his eye, maybe even going down his cheek a little. What with the glare from the TV and all, it was hard to tell. But I think he might've been crying.

*

My mom and I went inside the trailer. The paramedics had left all the lights on, the furniture had been pushed around in all directions as they must've tried to make room for the stretcher and their oxygen equipment. You could see their boot prints all over the floor where they had tracked mud in from the yard. The bedroom was in even worse shape. The sheets were tangled up with the plastic tubes from my dad's oxygen tank, there were pillows and clothes everywhere and the sliced-open plastic containers from which the paramedics had pulled out equipment to try to save my dad's life.

My little sister, who was nine, was next door at my grandparents' house, and my mom wanted to straighten up before we called over there to tell her about Dad. We started picking up. We took the sheets off the bed and put them in the washer. We picked up the trash left behind by the paramedics. We swept up the clods of mud from the kitchen floor and we moved the furniture back to where it was supposed to go. We cleaned the house. It was all we knew to do.

Part Three
2000s

12.

Isaw my mother for the first time in eighteen years when she came to live with my grandparents in Folsom. I was twenty years old. Her coming there was not expected, nor did I get the impression that it was wanted by my grandparents, who had kept a safe distance from her since she had given me up for adoption. My grandfather would mail her a monthly check, but she was never invited to our house for holidays or special occasions. My grandparents visited her at her trailer in Waveland maybe once or twice a year. It was March of 2000, my dad had been dead for barely three months, and our whole family was still in a sort of numb shock, not just from his death, but from the events leading up to it as well.

I got the phone call from my mom telling me that Susie was at my grandmother's house and that she wanted to see me. They told me that her husband, Bobby, had been in a terrible accident. He was beaten outside of a casino in Gulfport by four men who robbed him, bashed in his skull with their boots and a baseball bat, and dragged his nearly-dead body to a drainage pond in the woods, which was known to be filled with alligators. Luckily, someone happened to be walking back there the next morning and found Bobby's body before any alligators could get him, but he was in bad shape. Susie had called my grandparents, hysterical, when she heard what had happened. She told them that Bobby was in a coma, that he might not make it, and that she needed their help, so they brought her back to their house in Folsom. It had all happened so fast that it was hard to process, and although

I had fantasized about meeting my mother for my whole life, now that it was happening—and under such horrible circumstances—I didn't know how to react. I just told my grandmother that I would be right over.

Their house was only a short walk away from the trailer where I had grown up—they had moved from New Orleans a couple of years after us and built a house on the other side of the property from where our trailer was. The anticipation and fear, the sense of excitement that I felt as I walked across the gravel walkway, was unreal. I kept wondering if my mother was looking out of one of the bay windows as I approached the house. I imagined her running outside to greet me, embracing me like they do in the movies, as if no time had passed between us. But instead, no one came out.

I walked up to the back door and knocked, trying to see in through the window where my mother was, but I couldn't see her. I opened the door and walked into the kitchen, telling my grandmother hello like I usually did, as though nothing was out of the ordinary. Then I saw my mother standing next to the table in the living room. She had just come out of the bathroom, presumably, and now there she was. She was skinnier than I had imagined her, her large glasses making her face appear gaunt and sunken in. She didn't approach me at first, but then I walked over to her and hugged her. She was wearing a navy blue men's golf shirt and the fabric was rough against my skin. Her arms went around me and I could feel her ribs and I could smell her body odor. She smelled strongly of sweat, like a man. I could see the sweat stains under her arms, but it was not nearly as bad as she would start to smell years later.

My mother kept hugging me, and I could feel the rest of the people in the room watching us, but there were really no powerful emotions like I had imagined there would be. It just felt as though no time had passed since I had last seen her. That's the only way I can describe it. It was as though I had known her and seen her every day for the past eighteen years.

After my mother held me to her for a minute or so, she pulled away from me and started rubbing my face like a blind person would do, feeling every curve, every bone in my skull. Then she rubbed my hair with her skinny, jaundiced fingers. "Man, look at this thick hair you got," she said. "Just like me with all this thick hair. Look at you." I felt like a baby monkey being picked at by its mother for nits. She kept saying, "Man, I can't believe it. Look at you. Man, you're so tall. Gretchen, look how tall he is. Mom, he's so tall. Look at him."

I didn't know what to say. I didn't say anything.

My mother didn't cry; instead she laughed. Like her emotions were all mixed up. I can't imagine how she felt. Years later she would tell me that she had had recurring nightmares in which I was a baby and someone was pulling me from her arms. As much as she would try to find me in those horrible dreams, she never could. She would wake up sweating and crying, she said.

After a few minutes of standing there with everyone in the room staring at us, my mother asked me if I would play the piano for her. She told me that she had heard I was good. I told her that I really wasn't that good, that I had taught myself how to read music, play a couple of pieces that I liked, but nothing beyond that. She wanted to hear anyway.

So we walked over to the piano at the corner of the den and sat down next to one another on the bench. She asked me what I knew how to play. I told her that I could play "Für Elise" and a little bit of "Moonlight Sonata," so she waited for me to get situated at the keyboard. Surprisingly, I was calm playing the piano for her, and I pounded out those dark chords on "Moonlight Sonata" like I imagined Beethoven himself doing: all passion, no concern for perfection or a missed note or two, which was good because I hit quite a few wrong notes. When I was done with the little stretch I was able to play from memory, my mother said, "Man, that sounds good. You really play with a lot of feeling. Not many people can do that."

"Thanks," I said.

Then I asked her if she would play something for me. She said that she hadn't played in years, but I told her that I didn't care. I wanted to hear her play. I had heard she was really good too.

My mother moved around on the bench some, rubbed her fingers on some of the keys. I could tell she was nervous. Then she started playing "Clair de Lune" by Claude Debussy, and she went through the whole piece by memory alone, missing maybe only one or two notes. It was beautiful. I could see my grandmother watching us suspiciously from the kitchen, calling out every now and then to my mother when she hit a wrong note, "Wrong note, Susie!" I knew that my grandmother would be jealous of me meeting my mother, but I hadn't imagined she would act this way. The dynamic I had tried to block out from my childhood was resurfacing already.

My mother and I visited well into the evening on that first night, eating dinner together with my grandparents, watching a movie while we all ate. I could immediately feel the tension rising between my mother and grandmother. They bickered like children, making sarcastic comments to one another, my grandfather sitting tight-lipped in his spot on the sofa, trying every now and again to change the subject. The movie *American Beauty* was on TV and we were watching that when a particularly graphic scene came on where one of the girl characters was grilling her friend about giving her boyfriend oral sex. My mother laughed hysterically the whole time at this, which, had she not kept it going for so long and so dramatically, I wouldn't have thought odd, but I could tell that her reaction was her attempt to cover up her discomfort at seeing this with me present.

When it started getting late and my grandparents were getting ready for bed, I kept trying to leave to go back home myself. I was tired and had to wake up early the next morning to go to school. It was my first semester back in college after dropping out two years earlier when I came dangerously close to what I thought was a nervous breakdown. This had been right around the time my dad started to get really sick, and I got a really bad stomach ulcer. As much as I didn't want to, I had to withdraw from my classes. But now I was back in college and my first class was at eight the next morning, so I kept telling my mother that I had to go.

We would make it as far as the kitchen door and then she would think of some other important question she just had to ask me. More often than not, it was a question she had already asked me five or six times before, but I was cautious of hurting her feelings or being rude, so I answered her again and again. My grandfather had gone to bed by now, and my grandmother had come into the kitchen several times to tell Susie to let me leave, but she just couldn't let me go. I could understand this, and I didn't want to upset her, so I kept standing there.

Finally, close to midnight I told my mother that I *had* to leave, that I really needed to get some sleep. She said okay, but as I was walking out of the door, her eyes started to roll back into her head and she collapsed onto the kitchen floor. She didn't fall so much as she just wilted there, hanging onto my clothes as she went down. Then she lay flat on her back and one of her legs and then her arms started to spasm. I honestly thought that she was having a seizure, that perhaps it had been brought on by the overwhelming feelings of seeing me, her son, for the first time in eighteen years. I called out to my grandparents for help, and they both came out of their bedrooms and started bending over Susie, telling her to try to get up. They didn't seem upset, just angry, and it was then I knew this was likely an act on my mother's part. It didn't stop me from being worried though.

After a while when my mother still wouldn't get up or respond, I grabbed the phone and called 911 while my grandparents went into their rooms to get dressed. I waited next to my mother and tried to talk to her. Her eyes were still rolled back in her head and fluttering and her legs and arms were tense and stiff as two by fours. In just a few minutes the fire truck from the volunteer fire department in Folsom was there, followed shortly by an ambulance.

The paramedics came inside and after trying to talk to my mother for a minute or two, looking at her and examining her, they helped me to stand her up and took her into the guest room where she was staying, and we put her down on the sofa bed. My mother still was not talking, her limbs and body were rigid, and her eyes were still fluttering and rolling back into her head. At some point she started to reach for a plastic Walmart bag that was on the night table next to where she was lying down, so I picked up the bag and handed it to her. It was half-full of little shards of light green grass, the grass she had told us she had been eating for the past few years.

Mixed in with this was a small Ziploc bag in which my mother had some pill capsules. She pulled the Ziploc bag out, opened it, her arms suddenly working for her now, and she pulled out one of the yellow capsules, broke it open, and started rubbing the liquid from inside of it on her lips, which started to turn a dark orange upon the application of whatever this stuff was. One of the paramedics asked her about it, but my mother didn't answer. Whatever it was, it seemed to work, as now my mother was almost instantly revived.

It still hadn't occurred to me that she could have been faking this entire ordeal, that all of this was a very dramatic ploy to keep me from leaving that night, but when I saw the frustration, the head-shaking and eye rolling of a couple of the paramedics, their lack of urgency, I knew that my mother had done this on purpose, that there was nothing wrong with her. She would later claim that she had been having seizures and strokes for the past fifteen years, and this was one of them, but she would also claim that she was going deaf despite the fact that she could hear me whispering from across the room, but only if I was whispering something of interest to her, that she was nearly blind—she would squint her eyes dramatically whenever you tried to show her something she didn't want to see; other times, she could see better than I could.

Whether it was protocol or whether they just wanted to make it worth their effort for driving all the way out to the backwoods of Folsom in the middle of the night on a Sunday, the paramedics insisted that my mother go to the Emergency Room to be checked out by a physician. Maybe they were concerned by how underweight she was, or maybe they were worried about her mental health. I don't know, but I was able to help them convince her to get in the ambulance by saying that I would ride to the hospital with her.

I watched them put my mother on a gurney, wheel her out of the house, down the driveway to where the ambulance was parked, and then I watched them place her in the back of the ambulance, the whole while she was sitting up and looking nervously at me to make sure I was really going to come with her. I assured her that I was going to get in the ambulance with her, and once she was secured I climbed in and sat on one of the benches next to a paramedic. My grandfather followed us to the hospital in his car.

When we got to the hospital and to the Emergency Room, my mother was placed in a triage unit right next to the one where I had seen my dad's dead body just a couple of months before. And then we waited. Hours went by and several doctors came in the room, but my mother refused all of the tests they wanted to perform, refused to be admitted, telling them that she just needed a new pair of glasses. My grandfather, who I later learned had been through similar ordeals with my mother countless times over the course of her life, just sat in the corner, tight-lipped, angry, and tired. It was almost three in the morning.

The end result was that my mother left the Emergency Room against the doctor's orders, no tests were given, no recommendations, no answers, just the beginning of what turned out to be a series of frustrations and inconveniences that ultimately resulted in anger and a sense of hopelessness and despair on my part.

When we got back to Folsom, I had just enough time to splash some cold water on my face, get a cup of coffee and get in my car to drive to school. I had already dropped out of college once, and I wasn't planning to do so again. My eyes were red all day, and I kept nodding off in class, barely able to concentrate for not only being exhausted but for thinking about the first day I had met my mother and what was yet to come.

13.

The next few weeks weren't much different. My mother tried to dominate my time, encroach on my space, had episodes of near violent conviction about how I was "taken away from her," how unfair her life had been. She would get so riled up on these occasions that she would poke at my forehead with her yellow finger, staring into my face with her bulging eyes, and repeat over and over how much she loved me. It was uncomfortable to say the least, and I started to spend less time around her. I started to feel drained both emotionally and physically. *This is my mother, for Christ's sake, not my child*, I thought. Then I began to distance myself.

She would try to get my attention by lying to me, telling me that she was terminally ill, that she was going blind, deaf, had cancer. I stopped believing anything she said, but once she was able to convince me to take her to the little supermarket in Folsom to pick up some "personal items." She told me that she really needed them and that my grandmother refused to take her. It would only take a minute, she said. Please, she said. And so I gave in.

I drove her to Saia's, the only little grocery store in Folsom, and I waited in the car while she got out and went inside. I asked her if she even had any money and she assured me that she did. I waited. And waited. After about ten minutes, I got out of my car and started walking over the pea gravel lot toward the sliding doors at the front of the store, where a couple of men were loitering next to the Coke machines and the pay phones. As soon as I got close, I saw my mother ambling out of the store, her hands empty, as though she were completely hammered.

I walked over to her to grab her arm, as she looked like she needed help walking all of a sudden, but as soon as I got close, she wilted down toward the sidewalk—just like she had done on the night I first met her. But this time I wasn't buying it. I picked her up and started dragging her back to the car. I didn't ask if she was okay, could feel my lips tightening over my teeth just like my grandfather's had done so many times when he was mad but couldn't express it, and even when a couple of the store clerks came running outside to see what was the matter, I kept dragging my mother to the car. Everyone was looking at me as though I were some sort of criminal or an abuser of some kind, but I put my mother in the car, told the store employees and the loiterers—also now coming toward us, seemingly full of joy and excitement at something actually *happening* in their day now—that my mother was fine, that she did this sort of thing all the time. I told them that I would take her home and put her to bed. There was nothing wrong.

As I drove away, though, I could still see the group of people standing outside the store, looking suspiciously as I pulled out of the small parking lot, one of them with a pad and pencil, probably writing down my license plate number. *Just in case*, he must have thought. *Just in case*.

A couple of days later, between juggling both school, work, and my mother, I walked out to the front porch of our trailer to get some air and relax on the swing. My brother was sitting out there smoking and we talked for a few minutes before I heard the sounds of my mother screaming and cursing from across the way where my grandmother's house was. My brother pitched his cigarette and got up, about to run over to help. But I stopped him. I didn't know what was going on, but something told me to just let it happen. I don't know why I wasn't more worried about my grandparents' safety or even my mother's, but there was something in me that just couldn't react. I was numb.

My brother reluctantly stood by, anxious to run over to help, and then we could see my grandfather putting my mother in the backseat of his car and driving away, very quickly. We finally both walked over to my grandmother's house and she told us that my grandfather was taking Susie back to Waveland, that Susie had pulled a butcher knife on her and tried to stab her with it. She looked relieved, not just to be alive, but that Susie was finally gone from her house. We never called the police.

Eventually my mother ended up living in a small camper that my grandfather purchased for her and paid one of Susie's neighbors to keep in his back yard. He was putting out about a thousand dollars a month to keep Susie tucked away, as she had been for so much of my life until her husband was nearly killed. The next few months I heard updates about my mother, how her husband was slowly recovering, how she was visiting him in the hospital, helping him to get rehabilitated. He had to re-learn how to walk, speak, and to remember who he was, who my mother was, everything. It was a clean slate. I also heard how the neighbor, Melvin, whose back yard Susie was living in, had tried to rape her. When she made the accusation against him, the man was so mad that he kicked her off his property, keeping the camper as payment for his troubles, so Susie eventually moved back into her trailer next door to her mother-in-law, her slowly-recovering husband at her side. As before, no one ever called the police. As I was slowly learning, and had probably suspected most of my life, matters involving Susie were swept up into a neat little pile—as neat as you could get it at least—and dropped into the trash. Hopefully, you wouldn't have to deal with it again. I myself wouldn't have to deal with it for a while, not seeing my mother again until my grandmother passed away seven years later.

14.

My grandmother's funeral was held in the same funeral home as my dad's had been some eight years earlier. My mother and her husband, Bobby, arrived in Bobby's little white pickup truck and were both dressed in jeans and dirty sweatshirts. Susie's hair, much longer than it had been the first time I met her, was unkempt and tied back with a rubber band, and she was wearing a pair of men's hiking boots. Some of our family members who hadn't seen my mother in quite a long time came up to her and talked to her for a while. Bobby stood off to the side with his hands in his pockets and looked nervously around the room. I walked over to him and started talking to him, asked how he had been doing since the hurricane. I knew that they had a rough go of things trying to rebuild and clean up their land. They had lived in a FEMA trailer park near the coast for a while, then had a small FEMA trailer placed on their lot. Eventually, a church group came out from somewhere up north to help them build a raised cottage.

Bobby told me that things were going fine. He said that he was nervous about the government's plans to create more hurricanes like Katrina—maybe even worse—with the satellites that were strategically placed throughout the Gulf of Mexico for this very purpose. He said that he had been reading a lot lately how Japan had purchased the United States and was currently attempting to move its citizens away from the coastlines in order to set up their nuclear arsenals (the hurricanes were part of this plan).

I listened to him with sincerity, with interest in what he thought and believed. I knew that no one else took him seriously, that no one really liked him. But I also knew that he had loved and stuck with my mother for all these years, and I respected him for that. I knew firsthand how difficult she could be.

While I delivered the eulogy for my grandmother, I could see my mother pacing around the back of the funeral home, whispering to some of the attendees, laughing quietly. I didn't take offense to this, but I wonder if it upset her to hear me saying these nice things about my grandmother, with whom I know she had a tumultuous relationship over the course of her life. After the funeral was over, the procession moved to Folsom and ended at my grandmother's house, where we all ate and visited.

At some point, my mother had gotten a hold of a bottle of wine and started drinking. Within less than twenty minutes, she was acting erratically, her eyes bloodshot and bulging, her laughter carrying across the room. Bobby was following cautiously behind her, trying to get the cup of wine from her, but she kept pushing him away, going around the house and asking everyone the same questions over and over. Eventually she came to where I was sitting on the sofa and started pointing her finger in my face, acting accusatory and angry. I tried to ignore her. Someone pulled her away. I could see everyone in the den staring at me, both family and friends of the family, whispering to one another. They all knew that this woman was my mother, and somehow it seemed that her behavior was a reflection of me, who I was.

Of course, it wasn't, but the implication still stung. When my mother's behavior started to get completely out of hand, she was cursing and getting louder and louder with each passing minute, Bobby was finally able to get her in the truck and they left. She would tell me years later—after Bobby was dead and she was living with me and my family after trying to kill herself and after being committed to a mental institution—that she went back to her trailer in Waveland after her mother's funeral that day and drank for two weeks straight, non-stop, case after case of cheap beer and wine. She said she totally obliterated herself. Not because she was upset by her mother's death, she said, but just because she could.

Part Four
Now and Beyond

15.

My mother tried to commit suicide when her husband of nearly thirty years was diagnosed with an inoperable brain tumor. We had known about the diagnosis after visiting with her and speaking with the doctors, so we were all worried when Susie wouldn't answer her phone one evening. My mom had called numerous times and kept getting the answering machine so she eventually called me and asked if I would drive out to Waveland to check on Susie. I said okay, that once I got off work, I would drive out to Mississippi to check on my mother.

I walked up the steps leading to her raised trailer and knocked on the door. No answer. I knocked several times, harder and with more force each time, but still no one was answering. Susie's tiny dog was barking and the lights inside were on, but she wasn't coming to the door. I called my mom from my cell phone and told her what was going on and she said she would try calling Susie's house again. We hung up and then I could hear the house phone ringing, the answering machine clicking on, and my mom's voice calling out to Susie. Then I finally heard Susie's voice. It was very low, scratchy-sounding, and she was asking for water. She kept saying she was thirsty.

By this time, one of Susie's neighbors was pulling up to check to see if Susie was all right. I told him what was going on and he called 911. A few minutes later, the fire department arrived, along with an ambulance and several police cruisers. They, too, knocked on the door, calling out to my mother, but we could only hear her asking, in a low moan, for water.

One of the firefighters took a long ladder and climbed up to several of the windows to see if he could spot her, but he was unable to see her through any of the windows. They told me that the only way they could get in was to pry open the front door, but that they would need my permission to do so. I told them to do whatever they had to do to get inside.

I stepped aside and watched as one of the firemen used a black crowbar to rip the door apart from its frame. When they were inside, I followed behind them to find my mother lying on the kitchen floor, just under the table in a puddle of her own urine and feces. Her little dog, malnourished and without water, was scampering nervously over her prostrate body and barking at all of the strangers who were now in his territory. The paramedics bent over her and started asking her questions, peeling back her eyelids and pointing a light into her eyes. She was hardly responsive. I had seen my mother like this several times before, and it had always been a ploy for attention, so I wasn't overly distraught by this sight, nor did I feel any real emotional connection to her at that time to be truly upset.

The paramedics told me that she was definitely dehydrated and that they would need to take her to the ER to get some electrolytes and to run some tests on her. I told them that would all be fine and so they put a brace on her neck, strapped her to a gurney, and wheeled her outside and to the ambulance. I didn't even tell her goodbye.

Her neighbor, John, suggested that I take Susie's little dog, Toby, home with me, and then he helped me nail a piece of plywood over Susie's broken door. I drove back to my house, where my wife and two children were already asleep, I placed the dog in the garage (he reeked so horribly of urine and feces that I simply couldn't let him in the house), gave him some food and water, and went to sleep.

The next morning, a nurse from the ER where my

mother had been admitted called me and started to ask me questions about whether or not my mother had ever abused benzodiazepines before. Truthfully, I didn't even know what those were, didn't know much about my mother's history then either, so I told him "no." He said he was asking only because there was a large amount of "benzos" in her blood work. Then he said that he would call me back later. I remember putting down the phone, standing in the backyard for a minute or two, then calling back and asking the nurse what exactly he was trying to tell me with this information.

I asked if my mother had purposely taken those drugs to try to kill herself. He paused for a minute, then told me that, yes, the amount of drugs in her system pointed toward an intentional overdose. In other words, my mother had tried to end her own life. I didn't know it at that moment, but this would be the beginning of my foray into the dark world of mental hospitals, courts, lawyers' offices, social workers' offices, police stations, and group homes. My life as I had known it and made such an effort to forge for myself and for my family was about to change beyond anything I could have ever comprehended.

I began getting regular updates from the hospital on my mother's condition. They told me that she was improving, but was currently being held in the Intensive Care Unit since the amount of drugs she had taken and the severe dehydration had caused her kidneys to start shutting down. Further, her leg muscles had started to atrophy, causing small muscle fibers to get into her blood stream, which if not monitored carefully, could cause her to have further organ damage and blood clots. They wanted me to come to the hospital as soon as possible to see her and start making a plan for her release. It seemed too soon to be speaking of release, but with no health insurance, and since neither Susie nor I was in any position to pay for the services they were providing, the hospital seemed eager to get my mother out of their care as soon as possible.

I spoke with a social worker and told her of my mother's situation, how she lived in squalor in a trailer that had been flooded by Hurricane Katrina, how she lived with her husband, who was himself mentally unstable, abusive, and who had recently been diagnosed with an inoperable brain tumor. He was given about a month to live. I informed her that living with me would not be an option since, even though this was my mother, I had a wife and two small children whose safety I had to think about. I told her that I hadn't even seen my mother in years, and prior to that, I had gone most of my life without seeing her. She was almost like a stranger to me.

The social worker started to talk about group homes, institutions, involuntary commitment, and eventually suggested my mother be sent to the Crisis Stabilization Unit in nearby Gulfport. There, she said, my mother would get a proper physical and mental evaluation, and a further determination would be made from there. By this time, I had made the one-and-a-half hour drive several times to visit Susie in the hospital. She had been moved from ICU to her own room, but she was still unable to walk without the aid of a walker. All she could say was that she just wanted to go back home.

The social worker, Jane, suggested that I obtain conservatorship over my mother so that it would be easier to have her committed to the state's custody, in addition to being able to sign papers on her behalf regarding decisions that would, without a doubt, need to be made. I spent hours on the telephone and in lawyers' offices, social security offices, and eventually a courtroom, where I had to testify in front of a judge and a closed-circuit television on which my mother appeared from where she was now being held at the Crisis Stabilization Unit. She was able to see me in the courtroom, and I was able to see her, nervous and standing next to a podium that came up to the middle of her chest as she gripped its sides and fumbled around for the words that might make the judge let her go.

But she just made her case even worse. What with her wild hair and bulging eyes, her repetition of nonsensical phrases and her tapping of the podium and microphone (which caused a loud static pop in the courtroom each time she touched it), the judge, after shutting off the connection between my mother and us, said that in all his years of doing this he had never seen a case quite so clear in need of state intervention. It was one of the most difficult things I ever had to do and I cried and hugged the social worker on our way out of the courtroom. Then we waited for the judge to sign the papers to commit my mother to the state of Mississippi.

My mother ended up in a nice, quiet institution just near the coast in Gulfport, Mississippi. I visited her there several times and she was always happy to see me. This was really the beginning of our relationship as a mother and son. They had cleaned her up some, and the medication had kept her emotional state somewhat subdued, but she still exhibited some of her bizarre behavior. On one of my visits, she was soaking a sock in a small Styrofoam coffee cup, just dipping it in and out of the warm, dirty water. She didn't say much, just stared off into the small visiting yard where other patients were playing basketball or horseshoes with their relatives.

After being there for a couple of weeks, and after my gaining conservatorship over her, the private hospital could no longer afford to house her. She had no insurance, no money, no assets, and this was always the primary concern of her caregivers there, though I think they really wanted to help her. So, my mother was moved to a state institution in Purvis, Mississippi, about three hours north of Gulfport.

My wife came with me one Easter Sunday to visit my mother in Purvis, and I went one other time so that my mother could visit her dying husband in hospice. He was in Gulfport, and it was a day's worth of driving on the back roads of Mississippi to get her there.

We visited with Bobby for an hour or two, Susie held him and cried over him, his body already emaciated and a constant grimace of pain devouring his face. The doctors had shaved half of his hair when doing the biopsy on his tumor, but hadn't bothered to shave the other side. The hair he had was greasy and was hanging over his ears and across his cheeks in wispy black waves. Bobby had always been clean shaven, but now he had a thick mustache and goatee, which actually looked good on him: the facial hair added some depth to his otherwise hollow cheeks and eyes, and it covered his thin, taut lips which themselves barely hid his orange, rotten teeth.

The room was dark and impersonal, and the TV mounted to the wall overhead was playing the movie *Blade Runner* on MUTE. It was the scene when the toymaker comes home to his lonely apartment to find the android, Pris, hiding among his over-sized toy dolls and robots. I looked away from the TV and back down at Bobby. Susie was standing over him and stroking his hair, lifting up his arms and inspecting his hands and fingernails like she would a small child who had just been born or how an orangutan would inspect its young for nits. She had done this to me when I first met her. You could see the discomfort this caused in Bobby, though, for he tried to pull away or move but he simply didn't have the strength to.

I told Susie that Bobby looked uncomfortable, that she should stop moving him around like that, but she didn't listen. It was as though she were trying to find a solution to the cancer that was eating away at his brains, trying to understand how it got there, how she could possibly get rid of it.

Bobby's spindly legs stuck out from underneath thin blue hospital blankets like two waxy candlesticks. Susie lifted up his legs and inspected his feet. His toenails were long and pointy, thick and almost orange, and his toes curled in on each other as Susie stroked the bottoms of his feet with her pasty fingers, causing him to pull away.

I watched this, my mother inspecting the man who had once beaten her with a length of plastic PVC pipe, the same man who had told Susie to kill herself if anything should ever happen to him, that no one would ever take care of her without him being around. This was the same man who also drank a case of beer a day, who was beaten nearly to death outside a bar in Gulfport and had rehabilitated himself, only to be nearly swept away by the storm surge from Hurricane Katrina, but managed to hold onto a tree branch until the water went down, at which point he was finally able to walk, in his underwear, to a neighbor's house and get some help.

My mother wept over Bobby, and I looked at her as she hunched over his body, the tight braid that someone in the mental ward had made of her feral gray hair, thick and dry as a horse's mane, heaving up and down with her small head as she cried over this man who had shaped her entire universe for the past thirty-some-odd years. He had controlled her to the point where she believed him when he told her that the reason they didn't have a television set was because the government was watching them through it, even when it was turned off. She believed him that the airplanes overhead were leaking chemical exhaust into the sky, that it misted down on all of us, causing cancer and mental retardation, a dumbing down of the masses.

I was mad at her for listening to him, mad at him for

taking advantage of her already-precarious mental state, and doing so for many years. He wouldn't let her eat save for some mung beans and wheat grass that he grew in a little garden in his yard, which he had made of rotten two-by-fours and torn Visqueen. He wouldn't let her bathe, exacerbating her already-irrational fear of taking baths, once telling her that bathing in one's own urine was the best, and most curative, form of bathing. But this she wouldn't buy. Of all the places she let her mind go, of all the things she forced herself to believe, my mother would not bathe in her own urine. So one day Bobby took a water bottle of his own warm piss and poured it over my mother's head, forcing her to scrub her hair and face with it, not even letting her change her grimy sweatshirt afterward.

When we first came to their house after Bobby had a massive seizure, bringing him down in the mud just outside their trailer, his rubber flip flops still in the dirt and a pile of feces where he had lost control of his bowels, we found Bobby's ninety-year-old mother closed off in a back bedroom, weighing just under sixty pounds, her frail hands quivering, her eyes sunken as far back as they could probably go inside of her skull, her skin pale and bruised.

After I called the ambulance to come get her, and while I was trying to keep my mother out of the room, I tried to feed this old woman who also reeked of piss and mold and whatever other foul smells hid in that god-awful place. Her mouth opened tentatively, like a baby bird's, as I tried to spoon some mashed potatoes and pear slices in their syrupy juice for her to eat. She devoured it. I lifted a carton of apple juice to her chapped lips, let her sip from the tiny straw. At one point, she stopped and asked who I was. I told her that I was Susie's son. She still looked bewildered, utterly confused. She asked me if she was dead, if she was in heaven. I told her that she was very much alive and that she was going to be all right.

When the paramedics arrived, my mother was pacing around in the small little room that passed for a den, mumbling to herself and saying over and over that it wasn't her who starved the old woman like that. She kept saying that it was Bobby who had done this, that he was trying to keep her alive this way, the best way he knew how, by not eating. He believed that all food caused cancer, and his mother's living to such a late age was proof that he was right. He was keeping her alive, he thought. My mother, I think, instinctively knew that this was wrong, which is why she was so nervous at the thought of the authorities finding the old woman like this.

But she also wasn't completely innocent. Not only was she complicit in the deterioration and malnourishment of her mother-in-law, whom she admits she could not stand, but once the paramedics removed the woman from the bed, I noticed that the dingy sheets were pocked with dried blood, some stains as big as my fist, some reaching up to the lumpy pillow where the woman's frail head had rested. When I asked my mother about this, she admitted to slapping the old woman a few times, but following up with saying that the old woman deserved it because she never stopped complaining.

It was then I understood the almost evil-sounding way in which the old woman croaked out, "This is good for you," when she saw my mother hunched over, leaning against the stained wall in anguish at hearing the news that Bobby had an inoperable brain tumor and would likely not live another month. I don't think Elaine knew it was her own son in peril, or if she did, maybe she was so mad at him for what he'd done that she didn't care.

Despite all of these almost unthinkable things I had heard about him, I still felt compassion for this man who was dying right there before me, and his grieving wife, who was my mother, given a day's leave from a mental institution after a failed suicide attempt, to come here and visit him. It was one of the saddest things I have ever seen, I think. I leaned over him, took his hand in mine, and I told Bobby then, right close to his ear, that I would take care of Susie. I told him not to worry. The only thing he said was "thank you" and then I heard him tell my mother that he loved her and that he was sorry for everything he had done. I couldn't hear anything else he tried to say, as it all came out in a low whisper that sounded gravelly and strained.

I don't think that anyone else ever visited him there in that hospice where the poorest people in Mississippi went to die, often alone, in the dark, the blue light from the TVs overhead washing down over their thin skeletons sheathed with rotting flesh, a constant stream of morphine dripping into their veins until their bodies finally began to shut down, to die piece by piece. No one but the nurses ever witnessed Bobby's final suffering, his last days. He died not seeing a familiar face. It was as though he never even existed.

When Bobby finally died, my mother was still in the hospital in Purvis, and I called to let her doctors know. They said they would tell her the news. Later, when they called me back, they told me that when my mother heard of her husband's passing, she fell onto the ground and would not move for almost an hour, maybe longer. She had become catatonic.

Bobby's remains then became my responsibility. As conservator, I was to make all of these decisions, and with no money to his name, his only option was to be cremated at a small funeral home in a very low-income neighborhood that seemed to specialize in respectfully dealing with the remains of the poor and of the unwanted. His ashes, to this day, have gone unclaimed. They are in a wooden box inside a cabinet in my garage.

16.

Susie was released from the hospital in Purvis three weeks later. The only conditions of her release were that she continue to take her medication and that she have a place to live for a couple of days until her affairs were all in order. With some reluctance, I offered to let her stay with me until she got on her feet. Despite warnings from family members and other relatives of how dangerous my mother could be, I just couldn't turn her away. After all, she was my mother, and even after so many years, I felt a deep love for her that only a biological child can have for his birth parent. It's a powerful bond.

The first night she stayed at my house, I let her sleep in my daughter's room, and I had both of my kids sleep in the room with my wife and me. I knew this wasn't going to be easy, and this was quickly confirmed on that first night when I was awakened by my mother talking loudly to her now-deceased husband. She kept telling him to stop, to go away, to leave her alone. I knew that she wasn't talking in her sleep because I could hear her in the den. It was at that moment all the pieces came together: one of my kids' toys, a toy that had been broken for months and that would occasionally start playing nursery rhymes at odd intervals, started to go off in my son's room. I was used to the toy doing this occasionally and had meant for a while to put it out in the shed where we wouldn't have to hear it, but I just hadn't gotten around to it.

My mother thought that it was Bobby pressing the button on the toy, and by the time I went out into the den to move it, she was pacing around nervously and was visibly disturbed. She was a little heartened to learn that I heard it as well, and she tried to laugh it off, but I knew that was a bad start to her stay here. I took the toy outside, put it in the shed, and shut the door. Then I went back into my room with my wife and children and tried to go back to sleep.

My mother's three-day visit quickly unfolded into three weeks. She was not ready to go back to her trailer in Waveland, so I kept giving her more time. I even enjoyed her company some of the time she was here. Despite her erratic behavior and poor hygiene, she is a very intelligent person, and it was interesting to hear her perspective on stories that I had grown up hearing about. Once I was able to get her over her fear that someone was watching her through the television set, we watched *Dead Man Walking* together. That was a blessing that I never thought would happen. But it wouldn't last.

Rosenblum Mental Health Center is located a couple hundred yards away from the interstate, tucked away behind a few industrial buildings and fronted by a large field of overgrown weeds and trees. I was supposed to take my mother there for a follow-up visit after her release from the hospital. She reluctantly agreed to go, but I could tell that she was nervous about it. I told her that she didn't have anything to worry about, that it was just routine, and since she had been in compliance with everything so far save for continuing her daily regimen of anti-psychotic medication, there should be no reason for her to worry.

When we got to the health center, there were groups of people standing outside in the parking lot. They were smoking, talking on cell phones, pacing around by the entrance, waiting for their turn to see a doctor or social worker. Susie and I went inside and I signed her in, gave the receptionist what information I had, and then she handed me a metal clipboard with a stack of paperwork to fill out. I could tell

that my mother was too frazzled to do any of this herself—
she kept getting up from her chair, going to the bathroom,
repeating countless times how she didn't think she should
be here, and a couple of times she even walked outside and
got in the back of my truck, telling me that she wanted to
leave. But still I persisted. I felt it was my responsibility as
her conservator to make her keep this appointment.

I filled out the forms as honestly and precisely as possible.
I stated how my mother had been hospitalized recently
after a suicide attempt, how she had been diagnosed with
schizophrenia first in her teens and then again more recently.
I wrote about her husband, now dead, the alcoholism, the
physical and emotional abuse she endured. At some point,
though, my mother came from outside and sat next to me.
She asked me what I was writing. I let her glance at the form,
but she took the clipboard from me and started reading it.

"Aww, no, man," she was saying. "This isn't right."

"Susie, give it back."

"No no no no," she said. "Let me see that."

She took the pen from me and started scratching through
what I had narrated. She tore through the forms with the
pen so that the paper started to rip and the ink bled through
onto the sheets below. Then she started to scrawl the words:
"depressed, nervous since my husband died OF BRAIN
CANCER!!!" onto the form.

She handed the clipboard back to me.

"Great, Susie," I said. "Now they're going to think you're
really nuts."

"Let's just go," she said. "I don't need to be here."

"You have to keep this appointment, Susie. I told them
I would take you, and I'm the one responsible. We're not
leaving."

I got up and brought the clipboard back to the receptionist,
explaining to her what my mother had done, only to look

back and see my mother leaving again. She ran out of the front door and into the parking lot.

"Can someone please see her?" I said to the receptionist. "She's not going to stay much longer."

"Okay," the receptionist said. "I'll get someone out right away."

We had already been waiting for almost an hour by this point, but now a doctor came out to the waiting room where I was standing. My mother was still outside.

"Do you think you can get her in?" he asked me.

"I'll try," I said.

I went outside and coaxed my mother back in by telling her that the doctor was ready to see her, that it wouldn't take long, and then we would be able to leave. I believed what I was telling her. She said all right and followed me back inside.

The doctor was still waiting there. He introduced himself to my mother and asked her to follow him to the back. He told me to wait where I was. I sat down. I was looking out of the window at some people who were milling around my truck when the doctor came back out and asked me to come with him. I got up and followed him through a small door which opened into a long, white, narrow hallway that was lined with doors on both sides. He turned into one of the first doors on our right and went behind a cluttered desk where he sat down and looked up at me, nodding for me to sit as well.

Once I was seated, he asked me to tell him about my mother. So I told him the things I had written on the form on the clipboard earlier, the things my mother had scratched out—how she had been hospitalized after a suicide attempt, how she had been diagnosed with schizophrenia, how she had been abused. I told him that she was upset about having to come here but that she would probably be better when she got back home, meaning my home, of course.

"Well, she's not going home," he said.

I looked at him. I didn't say anything.

"We can't let her leave like this. We've been watching her for a while, and she's not in stable condition. We've already filled out an OPC (Order of Protective Custody) on her. Someone from the Sheriff's office will be here soon to transport her to a facility."

I didn't know what to say. I was surprised, but I was not surprised. This felt wrong, but it also felt like the right thing to do. I was confused, shocked.

"So what do I do?"

"You can just go back home. Try not to worry. You've done enough. Take the day off."

"I probably should tell her goodbye then?"

"No, sir. That would be a bad idea. We'll take care of her."

I started to walk out of his office, looked down that long white hall, imagined my mother locked in one of those rooms back there, probably thinking I had set her up, that I had betrayed her. Then I went back into the waiting room and told the receptionist what had happened and that I wouldn't be needing to schedule a follow-up appointment. She looked surprised, said "okay," and then I went back out to my truck and drove home in a sort of daze.

When I got home and my wife asked where Susie was, and it hit me what had just happened, I started crying as I tried to tell her that they just took my mother away again. I explained what had happened and now my wife was just as confused as I had been. A while later, I started getting phone calls from psychiatrists at other hospitals in the area, presumably as my mother was being moved around until a bed opened up for her somewhere.

I repeated in detail to each doctor my mother's psychological history—what little I seemed to know since

I hadn't even seen her for most of my life—and then they seemed to be writing the information down, thanking me afterward, then telling me someone would be in touch soon. It was utterly surreal.

Eventually someone called me from a hospital in Bogalusa to inform me that my mother would be staying there while they evaluated her. They told me she may be there for a couple of days or a couple of weeks, that it really just depended on how well the evaluation went. So I was surprised when someone called me the next morning while I was at work to tell me that I could come pick my mother up. They were discharging her, having found no reason to commit her any longer. I told them that I would be there in a couple of hours.

The back roads from Slidell, Louisiana, where I was working at the time, to Bogalusa can take you a couple of hours to wind your way down. They are narrow, curving roads with tall pine woods on either side, log trucks speeding around the curves at various intervals and the occasional trailer set back off into the woods, but otherwise there's nothing.

When I got to Bogalusa, with the smell of the paper mill and the exhaust from the smokestacks visible in the otherwise cloudless sky, I drove around the decrepit town past the abandoned houses and weeded lots, driving over the cracked roads until I found the hospital where my mother was staying. I went inside and took an old, orange elevator up to the second floor, where someone behind a caged partition told me how to get to the Behavioral Health Unit. I went down the musty hallway and pressed the buzzer on the side of the large metal door which locked the patients inside from the rest of the hospital. I could see through the glass window secured with chicken wire some of the patients milling around in their robes, their hair tousled, their incessant roaming endless and aimless.

A doctor came out from the door and I told him I was here for my mother, Susan Roberts, and he said that he would go inside and tell her. We never discussed her status, her well-being, any long or short-term plans. He just went back inside the locked unit to get her.

When my mother came out, she was holding her shoes in one hand and her shoelaces in the other. She had a Walmart bag in the same hand as the laces, and this contained her belt. She acted as though nothing was wrong. She sat down quickly in one of the chairs and started lacing up her shoes.

"How's it going?" I asked her.

"Good, fine. I just want to get the hell out of here."

"Why did they unlace your shoes like that?" I asked her.

"So I couldn't hang myself," she said. Then she looked up at me and laughed. "Crazy huh?"

My mother seemed in high spirits. It was as if I were picking her up from any place except a mental institution in Bogalusa, Louisiana, that we were going to go somewhere and do something fun and adventurous. I was just happy that she wasn't mad at me, that she didn't think I had set her up.

"Naw, man," she said. "Those people were assholes. I know it wasn't your fault."

She finished lacing her shoes, then stood up and put her belt on. She wadded up the empty Walmart bag, then took her discharge papers out of her pocket and threw them in the garbage can along with the bag.

"Let's get out of here, man," she said.

We walked down to the first floor, went outside into the sulfuric air, got into my truck, and drove through that desolate little town until we were on the highway again, the one that would eventually lead back home, where my mother would slowly deteriorate into a completely different person.

*

After my mother had lived with me for about six weeks, holing herself up in my daughter's room with her dog, Toby, locking the animal inside of the bathroom whenever she went outside or into the kitchen—otherwise, she would hold him wrapped tightly in a blanket as if he were a newborn child in a papoose—I had to call the police and have my mother recommitted to the hospital. Her behavior had simply gotten too much for me to handle. She would stick her dirty fingers in our food, eat peanut butter out of the jar with a spoon, placing the spoon in her mouth, scraping the contents off with her rotten, orange teeth, then putting the spoon back for another scoop of peanut butter. She ran her fingers along the edges of our milk, which she never drank, our half and half, which she also never drank, and she started to dig through our garbage, pulling out and saving wet napkins, soggy coffee filters, used notebook paper, toilet paper rolls.

She kept these things in my daughter's room, and the room and our entire house was starting to smell very bad. We covered the sofa cushions with blankets for when she sat on them so that we could pull off the blankets every couple of days to wash them. I had to keep my bedroom door shut so she wouldn't go inside and dig in my dresser drawers. She liked to wear my clothes. I had sympathy for her at first. She was my mother, after all, and there was a strange relief in my soul at having her living in my house, getting to know her. But there was also an anxiety that kept me awake nights, an anxiety I can't quite understand, even now.

I loved my mother, I still do. I think there is a natural connection between us that is unbreakable, unknowable, but one that I have to keep at a distance in order to stay well myself.

The morning I had my mother picked up by the police and committed to the mental institution for the second time in almost as many months was just like any other morning. I woke up, made coffee, started up my computer to check my messages for work. My mother was in the kitchen now, pouring herself a cup of coffee, holding Toby to her chest with a blanket wrapped tightly around him. She was taking little bits of dog food that she had spread out on the kitchen counter, dipping each piece into a cup of water, which itself was slowly turning the color of cardboard, then hand-feeding the animal each individual piece of food. She was still perturbed by how many teeth had been extracted from the dog's mouth while she was in the hospital in Purvis.

I had taken the dog to the vet after finding him malnourished and smelling of urine and rotten food, expecting the vet to want to put the dog down—he weighed about four pounds when I took him, you could see all of his ribs, he shook and quivered incessantly, and his toe nails had grown so long that he could hardly walk—but instead, the doctor was optimistic. He said that, despite Toby's physical appearance, he was not in terrible health. He needed to gain weight, sure, but other than that and a few rotten teeth, Toby would be all right. I agreed to let the doctor extract the teeth once Toby was well enough and had some more weight on him to be able to handle the anesthetic.

When my mother first came home with me, she immediately ran to the back door where Toby was jumping up and scratching the glass, waiting to see her. I fully expected him to run and cower away from her after being smothered by her so much and then experiencing a completely different life for the past six weeks at my house with my kids and our dog, Emma, but instead he went right to her, and she instantly zeroed in on his mouth, asking what happened to his teeth. No amount of rational explanation could satisfy her, and she refused to accept that feeding the dog soft, half-rotten bananas for years hadn't done harm to his teeth. Her logic was that the dog would choke on anything hard or crunchy.

I have to stop here and point out how similarly my mother treated me as a child, and how looking at that dog set off this deep well of anger and resentment inside of me, and that I often imagined how crippled I would have been had she been allowed to raise me my whole life. When I looked at that dog, I experienced a strange sense of *déjà vu*, as though I were watching myself being trapped and suffocated by my mother's twisted idea of love and caring.

So I was watching my mother feed Toby this way, and I was trying to ignore her as I did my work, but then she started asking me about my father-in-law, on whom she had a crush and which she made no effort to hide. She would sit next to him when we brought her with us to my mother-in-law's house, hanging on his every word, inquiring about his artwork and offering such exaggerated praise for everything he did that even I was embarrassed. After we went home, I had told her as much, and now, on this day, she wanted to talk about it again.

This is how my mother is. No particular subject is ever exhausted for her, as though a conversation or an event from thirty years ago happened just a couple of minutes prior, and she jumps into this conversation head first, giving her listener no time to adjust or get context for what she's about to say. When she's like this she speaks with a quickness and an intensity that can make your stomach ache, her eyes grow wide and wild, and her pupils dilate. She looks right at you, almost *through* you, and she repeats herself over and over.

On this particular morning she was asking me why I thought it was so inappropriate for her to like my father-in-law. For one, I told her because he was married, and two because it was just wrong. Plain and simple. But that wasn't enough. She kept going on about it. I was trying to work, trying to ignore her, but she kept talking, kept repeating the same questions, as if the answers to them were a matter of life or death. I don't know what happened then. I just snapped. I stood up from where I was sitting in front of the computer, screaming as loud as I could. Not really screaming words, just screaming. I had never been this out of control before, and it was frightening. My mother looked at me, then started to walk quickly away and toward the bathroom, where she closed the door and locked it behind her, telling me to leave her alone.

I couldn't though. I punched the wall next to the bathroom door, creating a giant hole in the drywall. I told her to come out of the bathroom. She did. Then I followed her outside to the backyard, where I continued to yell at her, listing what was probably more than thirty years of pent-up pain and frustration and utter confusion about my life and this woman who was my mother: the way she treated her dog, the way she treated and talked to me, the unconditional love that I knew she felt for me, though was only able to express in bizarre and overwhelming ways. It was all too much. Things had suddenly reached the breaking point.

I chased my mother out into the backyard and told her she had to leave. I was going to take her back to Waveland, she had lived with me long enough. I was tired of her fake illnesses, her throwing up in my hallway when she didn't want to leave the house with us, her erratic sleeping habits, her selfishness. I told her I was leaving for a while, and that when I got back, she had better be packed and ready to go. I am not proud of this. It was the worst side of myself that I had ever experienced, one that scares me to this day just knowing that it exists inside of me. I don't know if I can blame anyone for it either. It's just there.

When I left my house, I drove around screaming and punching the steering wheel. I was crying. I called my wife and told her not to go home just yet, that things had gotten really bad between Susie and me and that I didn't want the kids to see anything like I had seen as a young boy. It really was, like the cliché goes, as though history was repeating itself. Except now, I was no longer the helpless little boy hiding behind my grandmother's leg, I was my uncle jumping on the hood of the car with a murderous anger in my veins.

I didn't know what to do. I knew I couldn't take Susie home to her trailer in Waveland. There was no electricity there, she had no food, no money, nothing. As her conservator I could not leave her in a situation like that. I thought about all the behaviors that my mother had, all the things she did while living with me for six weeks, how she had refused to bathe, how she suffocated her dog, how she stole things from me and hid them in her endless piles of Walmart bags in my daughter's room, how she dug out my garbage, how she paced the kitchen at all hours of the night, talking to herself and to her dog, almost attacking me when I came out of the bedroom to ask her to go to sleep. She wasn't violent with me, she never yelled at me, but she would come at me with a slew of words and memories and would want to rehash old events for hours, all at the expense of my time, my family, my job, my emotional health and well-being. I thought about all of this and decided that I would have to have my mother committed again. I didn't know what else to do.

If you've never had to commit someone to the state before, here is how you do it: you have to call the Sheriff's office, then go to the Coroner's office and sign OPC (Order of Protective Custody) papers, stating that the person you're committing is a danger to either themselves or to others. Then you wait.

The police officer who was dispatched to take my mother

away asked me if I would follow him to my house, thinking it would be easier if I could help coerce my mother into the car with him. I told him I would do this. My stomach hurt and my hands were shaking as I drove back to my house. I didn't know what we'd find there. Would my mother still be there? Would she have tried to kill herself again? I didn't know. I kept thinking that it was a Saturday, for some reason, even though it was Tuesday, and even mentioned my concern to the police officer that the mental health unit in Hammond would probably be closed for the weekend, asking him where he was going to take her. He looked at me kind of strangely and reminded me that it was Tuesday, and that the place would surely be open. It was startling to be so disoriented by anger and fear and just confusion in general.

When we pulled up to my house, my mother was in the garage piling her bags next to the doorway, getting ready to leave as I had told her to do. As soon as she saw the police officer, she started to walk back inside, saying, "aww, no, man. Come on, don't do this. Aww, no." She said this over and over as the officer and I approached her. I couldn't look her in the eyes. I felt as though I were betraying her.

The officer told her that she had to get in the car, and that he was going to take her to the hospital. He told her that she was a suicide risk and that he could take her against her will if she didn't get in the car with him. He was very polite about it, very patient, and I'm grateful for that, but I still felt tremendous guilt for doing this. I still do. It pains me to write about it even now.

My mother complied, putting Toby back in the house, following the officer to the car, repeating over and over that she wasn't going to hurt herself, that she just wanted to go home, but the officer just drove away with her, not saying a word. To my knowledge she never took advantage of the moment to say I had yelled at her, punched the wall, chased behind her. She was faithful to me while I betrayed her.

I went back into my house, went into my daughter's room where my mother had been living for the past six weeks, and I started going through her bags. In them I found pairs of dirty socks and underwear, a bra, makeup containers that she had gotten from the mental institution in Purvis, coloring books, crossword puzzles, brand new tennis shoes I had bought for her but that she had never worn, even some things she had stolen from my children's rooms: some stuffed animals, some toy rocks. The sight of my kids' stuff in her dirty bags made me furious all over again and I started hauling the bags outside to the trash can, where I dumped everything she had.

Then began the slew of phone calls from doctors and social workers again, on which I had to cite the litany of problems my mother had, why she should be committed, why I wouldn't just let her go to her house in Waveland, the whole thing over and over and over. Finally, they said that they would transport her to a mental institution in Saint Charles Parish, and someone from there would eventually contact me. It was another whole week before that finally happened.

The doctor who finally called me wanted me to come out and speak to him in person about my mother. He told me that he had been observing her for the past week and was unable to come up with a sure diagnosis but felt pretty confident in saying that my mother was suffering from schizoaffective disorder. He told me how she rambled, how her perception of events and reality was not in line with how most people perceived things, how she refused to bathe, was thus malodorous, disorganized in her thinking, and had almost zero insight into her own condition. Weeks later, when I was able to read his notes on my mother, I could sense his own frustration in the way he wrote about her: "she repeats the same thing over and over and over and over," was one of the things he had scrawled on her records.

The hospital was a good hour and a half away from my house, and I had to take a day off of work to drive out there. The weather, as it always seemed to be when I was visiting my mother in a mental institution, was oddly beautiful. The sky was clear, maybe a tiny scud or two of clouds hovering overhead, the sun bright and warm, the air cool. I drove my little pickup truck down the interstate, shaken by the eighteen wheelers flying by me, until I eventually saw the cable-suspended structure of the Hale Boggs Memorial Bridge crossing over the Mississippi River, a half dozen barges, seemingly as large as football fields, lazily floating down the wide river and heading south toward the Gulf of Mexico.

At the sight of the high, narrow structure my stomach immediately started to tighten. I have been terrified of bridges ever since I was a child, have had recurring nightmares about them as far back as I can remember, and the thought of driving over this one was not a pleasant one at all. Ever since I was a boy, I've had this damned dream about driving over a bridge, only to crash off the side and into the water. The dream varies, but the basic premise is the same: I can always see the bridge from the distance as I drive down some circuitous city road, trying to find an exit that will take me away from the path of the looming structure. Often the thing is so high that I can't see its summit, just its black, snake-like curve ascending up toward the clouds, which are usually as white as the sun reflected in a shard of mirror or broken glass.

In this dream, the bridge has a steep gradient, so steep that you'd have trouble imagining how your car would even make it up without rolling backwards and crashing into the traffic behind it. Other cars are usually going up and disappearing into the clouds and no matter which direction I take I always end up right at the foot of it, unable to stop or turn around.

Sometimes in this dream I can see the water churning beneath the bridge, the waves lapping up over the guardrails and soaking the grated platform, hungry to wash away and swallow whatever is in its path. Over the years, I have been able to get out of the car I was in just at the foot of the bridge, only to find myself crawling on all fours up toward the summit, sometimes even shimmying on my stomach, such is the pure fear and dread I'm experiencing. But I can never stop. I can never pull away from the magnetic force that seems to be dragging me up to the highest point before the road again slopes down to the other side, to safety, comfort.

What has never varied in the twenty some-odd years I've been having this dream is this: I always, always end up sliding off the side of the bridge, feeling the wind sucked from my guts as I become completely weightless and plummet down toward the angry water. I wake up from this vision gasping for breath, sometimes even screaming out loud until I realize that I'm in my bed. What causes me to fall is often different. Sometimes a wave will reach up to the bridge and pull me down in its grasp, other times I simply slide off the side, pulled by some strange gravitational force. The times I actually drive up the slope of the thing I'll always skid off the road somehow, the last thing I see through the windshield as I brace for the impact is the dark, churning water below.

I've had dreams in which I manage to get underneath the bridge, standing in a long line of lethargic, silent people as they slowly make their way up a winding metal staircase that wraps around the concrete pylons like a strand of DNA. Once we're all at the top, we one by one fall from the bridge to our demise.

There have been variations in which I drive on an interstate for what seems like hours, following all of the signs carefully and methodically so that I will end up anywhere but on that bridge that is always sitting in the distance, waiting and rising up to unimaginable heights. No matter what I do, though, I always end up in its path. That never changes.

I've looked at pictures of the Orange Bridge in Port Arthur, Texas, and it makes my stomach hurt to see it. I've driven over the Huey P. Long bridge here in Louisiana, was actually in the car once when my dad was driving and got angry at someone who tried to cut him off and so he sped up to almost eighty miles per hour as we went up the steep, narrow two-lane bridge, the guardrails on either side little comfort when you know that your car could very easily go through them or even over them if you hit the concrete curb just right. I held on to the side of my door and looked down at my hands so that my dad wouldn't see me closing my eyes and know that I was scared. Being scared, or at least showing you were scared, was unacceptable to him.

Another time we were stopped in traffic just at the top of the Huey P. Long Bridge as a train was coming over it at the same time. (There's actually a train track that runs through the middle of the bridge and if you're crossing at the right time you'll find yourself either side by side with it as you go in the same direction as the train, or you'll feel as though the train's going to collide with you as you watch it inch closer and closer to your car as you go.) The weight of the train causes the entire bridge to shake and heave as though some giant hand is grabbing the pylons and shaking them from the barge-clogged Mississippi River below. It's a terrifying experience, one I've never wholly gotten used to, even after numerous trips over it and even since the bridge has recently been widened. There's something always ominous about the black and white sign hanging just at the foot of the bridge as you make your way up toward the entrance, something that always looks as though you're about to drive through a dark cave or a tunnel.

The significance of all of this, however, wasn't lost on me. Crossing this bridge seemed now symbolic in a way that is too obvious to need any further explanation, but I'll just say that going up that steep incline and reaching the summit—and from which vantage point I forced myself to look over the side at the sprawling river some one hundred and fifty feet below, the land before me flat and pocked with what looked to be new subdivisions filled with large houses—felt almost like looking at the quilted landscape from a plane on a clear day.

I always wonder what it is about me and bridges and these recurring nightmares that I have. I like to think that as I get older, I'll be able to safely get across the bridges in my dreams, no matter how strong the winds are or how turbulent the waters are below. I would drive up with no fear or apprehension and I would make the slow ascent toward the clouds, one hand on the wheel, feeling totally relaxed, completely comfortable. Then the white would start to envelop me like when you take off on an airplane, and I would just have to watch the black asphalt of the road to know where I'm going. The white dashes in the centerline would click off one by one like hyphens as I make progress in the dream. I would never flinch.

After maybe thirty seconds or so I would start to come down over the rise, the clouds already diminishing, the road smooth under my car's tires, a steady grip between the rubber and the warm asphalt. Then I would get to the other side, leaving the bridge behind me, a curved black line going up into the clouds just a still and silent picture in my rearview mirror. Maybe I'd turn the radio on then, put on some music as I drive the rest of the way to wherever it is I'm going, the road widening and fanning out into the horizon as I roll down the window, laying my foot down heavy and feeling the breeze in my hair just before I wake up to face the day, feeling at once whole and refreshed, ready for whatever's to come. This thought is both beautiful and terrifying. So was what I was about to do—see my mother for the first time in almost two weeks, but in the confines now of a locked room of the Behavioral Health Unit at St. Charles Hospital.

After I pulled up to the hospital, which was surrounded by the small houses of the working poor who couldn't afford to not live in the midst of a hospital and the sprawling, smoking factories that lined the river, I found a place to park and went inside. The Behavioral Health Unit was on the third floor, and I took an elevator up there, then went down the hall and pressed the buzzer on the side of the large metal door with its caged window. A nurse answered, and I told her who I was.

"Just a minute," she said. I went down the hall a bit and sat on one of the cushioned benches to wait, looking out of the large window at the beautiful sky, pocked as it was with smokestacks and refinery towers. I wondered if my mother had windows from which she could see the horizon, watch the sun go up or down. My mother loved nature, seemed to be most at ease when she was out in it. Like a child, she relished picking flowers or collecting rocks, shells, acorns, anything that had been cast off and forgotten: she could see its value, its inherent beauty. She once had me stop the car in the middle of the street so she could jump out and pick some flowers growing in the ditch.

After a few minutes the nurse came out of the heavy door and walked toward me. She sat down next to me and asked me a few questions about my mother, then told me to follow her inside the unit where I would be talking to the doctor about some things.

When she swiped her security card into the card reader beside the door, a buzzer went off overhead and something inside the door clicked and the nurse pulled it open. From the threshold I could see a few of the other patients milling around in their robes and pajamas, their hair messy and their eyes glazed over from strong medications. A couple of them looked at me excitedly, then started to approach me, their arms out as though they planned to give me a great hug, but then the nurse pulled me away into a side room where the doctor was sitting behind a desk. He was a young doctor, probably about my age, and I shook his hand and sat down. The nurse stood beside him at his desk as he flipped through his notes and turned to his computer several times as if preparing for a deposition.

First he wanted to know what I had in mind for my mother once she was released from the hospital. I told him I didn't have any idea. I had learned over the months that new laws did not allow for anyone to be indefinitely committed against his or her will, so that oftentimes group homes were the only solution. I'd already heard some bad stories from several of the social workers about so-called group homes that were really just small trailers with about twenty people living in them, the owner collecting all of their disability checks, only to provide them with the bare minimum of necessities in order to stay in compliance with the law. So not only were these places over-crowded, they were filthy and roach infested, dark and barely livable by most peoples' standards. A few of these, thankfully, I'd heard had been shut down recently.

The other option for people like my mother was homelessness.

"So what do you want to do?" the doctor asked me. "Your mother says she has a house in Mississippi and that she just wants to go back there."

"That place is not really in any condition for her to live in," I told him. "It doesn't have electricity, running water, it's a total mess."

"Well why do you care?" he said. I don't think he was trying to be difficult, but he really was curious why I would have any interest in my mother's well-being. This would be an obvious thing for most people in normal situations, but as he must have gleaned over the last few days, this situation was far from normal.

"It's just the right thing to do," I told him.

"But she didn't raise you, did she?"

"No," I said. It was as though since she hadn't been there for me, I should now turn my back on her. I had already done that once when I had her sent here. I didn't want to do it again. I couldn't let her live with me, though. Not only had it not worked the first time, but since I'd kicked her out to have her committed again, I had spoken with other family members and a couple of my mother's neighbors who had all told me stories about my mother: how she had tried to commit suicide several times in the past few years, how she and her husband would fight in their driveway, swinging pipes at one another, her screaming and a couple of times even running naked down the street. The police were called more than a few times.

I had heard how my mother would leave her husband for days or weeks at a time, much as she had done to me when I was a child, and how she would go off with other men on drinking and drug binges. She even told me a few of these stories herself, how once she had been in a car with a man she had met and they were so drunk that he flipped the car into the ditch, my mother's head going through the side glass. She said that she was so drunk that she just laughed hysterically until she finally passed out. She never did say how she got back home that night.

"Well it seems that your mom's only option would be to just go back to her house. You could have the electricity and water turned back on, couldn't you?"

"I could," I said. "But it's not really a safe place for her to live."

"Hasn't she lived there for almost thirty years?" he said.

"Yeah, but look."

I had come prepared for this. I didn't know how much good it would do but I brought pictures that I had taken of my mother's house to show to this doctor. I think I was hoping that he would see them and decide to keep her in the hospital indefinitely. This was a foolish thought, but I have to be honest that it did cross my mind.

I pulled out the envelope of pictures. In them you could see the trailer where my mother spent most of her time. Even after FEMA had put up a small raised cottage on one of her lots, she and her husband still liked to be in this moldy, rat-infested trailer which had no electricity save for what they siphoned into the place with a frayed extension cord, no running water, and was filled from floor to ceiling with garbage.

I showed him the pictures, watching him thumb through them and place them one by one on his desk, sucking his teeth and shaking his head slowly as the nurse stood behind him and looked with wide eyes and an "o" for a mouth. I could tell neither one of them had probably ever seen anything like this.

"What is this of?" the doctor said, showing me a picture of one of the trailer's bathrooms, in which the bathtub had been filled with empty water bottles and shampoo bottles, tubes of toothpaste. From the shower curtain rod hung moldy shirts and pants. Single shoes littered the floor and had it not been for the flash of the camera (which also illuminated the dirt floating in the air), the room would have been almost entirely dark.

"That's her bathroom," I said.

He didn't say anything, just kept flipping through the

pictures. In some of them you could see the exposed studs behind the waterlogged walls, where the sheetrock had simply come off like shed skin, the moldy, rotten wood behind it warped and covered with spider webs and the workings of frayed wires and rat-torn insulation, pink and hanging like a large furry tongue.

When he confronted my mother with these pictures later, she would tell him that the trailer in the pictures was used for storage and that she rarely went inside of it. This wasn't true, of course, and the doctor knew it, so he decided to start making calls to place my mother in a group home.

The next week, after fielding numerous calls from my mother's psychiatrist, directors of group homes in New Orleans, Baton Rouge, Houma, and even in some small towns in Louisiana that I had never even heard of, it was decided that she would move into a house in Baton Rouge, where I was to meet her and the owner to go over the details of her stay. Someone from the hospital transported my mother in a van to this new group home.

PSYCHIATRIC ADMISSION ASSESSMENT
HISTORY AND PHYSICAL

MENTAL STATUS EXAMINATION: She is disheveled. Eye contact, fair. Positive psychomotor retardation. She is malodorous and appears depressed. Mood, "Tired." Affect, blunted, flat at times. Thought processes, very vague, evasive, and circumstantial. Thought content, positive suicidal ideations per chart, however patient denies. Chart also reports positive auditory and visual hallucinations, but patient denies. Chart also reports positive paranoia. Judgment, poor. Insight, poor. Cognitive evaluation, she is alert and oriented x 4. She is able to name 5 out of 5 past presidents, which is above average. She is able to perform serial 7s which is above average. Her memory is 3 out of 3 immediate and 3 out of 3 at five minutes, which is above average. Her abstractions are intact and her remote and recent memory are also intact.

REVIEW OF SYSTEMS: As in history of present illness.

PHYSICAL EXAMINATION:

PROGRESS NOTE

PROGRESS NOTE: 6/10/2012

SUBJECTIVE: The patient still paranoid in denial about her house without utilities. The patient still states she is capable of taking care of herself although she showed extremely poor ADLs here on the unit with unkempt hair, wearing the same gown every day.

OBJECTIVE: VITALS: T-current 97.0, pulse 91, blood pressure 95/44, respiratory rate 20.

MENTAL STATUS EXAM: Disheveled, staring eye contact, minimally cooperative, still argumentative and with poor social cues and poor ADLs, slowed motor activity. Mood, "Better, well, about the same." Affect, still anxious and irritable, blunted. Thought process, still disorganized, loose associations, speech is clear. Thought content, still with paranoia, denies auditory/visual hallucinations, denies suicidal/homicidal ideations. Insight, poor. Judgement, poor

ASSESSMENT & PLAN: 60-year-old white female with-

1. SCHIZOAFFECTIVE DISORDER- Continue Seroquel XR 300-mg every at bedtime, Lithium 450-mg every at bedtime, Depakote 1200-mg every at bedtime and Invega Sustenna monthly. Will check labs in the morning.

SCH St. Charles Hospital	NAME: SUSAN ROBERTS	ADMIT DATE: 05/16/2012 ROOM #: 3010-A
REV 4/06	DICT PHYS: MD ATT PHY: MD Page 2 of 3	PSYCHIATRIC ADMISSION ASSESSMENT HISTORY AND PHYSICAL

My mother's commitment papers. She had been hospitalized for almost a month (05/16/12 – 06/10/12) by this point.

My mother, around two or three years old.

My mother at Fort Walton Beach, Florida, when she was around
fifteen.

My mother around sixteen or seventeen (I used to keep this
picture in my wallet when I was a teenager).

My mother probably around the time just before she became
pregnant with me.

This is the only existing picture of my mother and father
together (he is in the black suit sitting next to my mother in the
checkered dress). They are both around fifteen or sixteen here.
Their respective families were all friends so my mother and father
had known each other for some time. My mother is the only one
not smiling.

My mother and me, circa 1982-3.

My mother and me during Easter.

My dad wearing the green hospital scrubs he got when he nailed his hand into the rabbit cage and which he would wear until his last days. He is holding a fish he caught in a pond behind our house that, for some reason, he called "Walter."

One of the many notes my mother kept in a scrapbook for me. It reads: "'Mommy, I want a Kleenex.' David was looking at my maroon sweater and said 'blouse, nice blouse.' A few minutes after he got up at 9:30 I put on Channel 12 to see if Sesame Street was on—then he saw 'Read-a-Long' (quick storys [sic]) and said 'Cookie Jar' then he saw two laced-up boots! He must know how to read—amazing. In the den before his nap I told him Bryan [her nephew who would later become my step-brother] was rocked by Nanny [my mother's sister—the aunt who would later adopt me]—he said 'Bryan Amy I like you!'"

This note reads: "Oct. 15 '81—David found the book *The Sting* in the hall and said 'Sting, Sting.' Oct. 12—David said 'Excuse me' to Mimi [my grandmother] when he wanted to pass by the coffee table in the den. Sept. 26—David's first sentence (Jerry G. [a family friend] was drinking beer and suddenly David said 'I like it!'" (I still remember the old Lite Beer cans from which he drank, and I also remember him letting me taste it, frequently. This would turn out to be a bad omen for me later on in my life.)

"Nov. 23, 1981 David said 'Niven!' when he looked at a book by
D[avid]. Niven. Nov. 1981 David says 'adorable madly,' 'Mimi,'
'Mommy loves you—madly.' Before Sin. [Frank Sinatra] concert
Oct. – he brought Mimi a Sinatra book"

My mother's house in Waveland, Mississippi. (She would often
sleep in the tent on the back porch.)

Inside, den.

Bathroom.

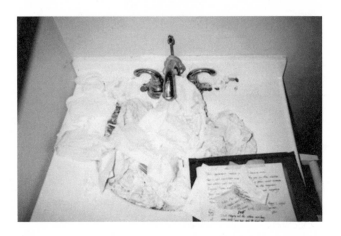

Bathroom sink. She keeps all of her sinks filled with toilet paper and tissues. (The notes on the counter are some of the ones she and her husband wrote back and forth to one another and tacked all over the walls.)

Second bathroom. (My mother says this is "storage.")

Kitchen. (The slant of the photograph is actually the way the trailer leans. It was knocked from its cinderblock foundations by the nearly thirty-foot storm surge from Hurricane Katrina on August 29, 2005.)

17.

The group home in Baton Rouge was an old house in a nice, quiet subdivision. The owner of the home, Ms. Angela, allowed the residents the freedom to come and go as they pleased, gave them the responsibility to purchase their own groceries, work out transportation with the public bus, keep the house and themselves clean, and follow a few other basic rules. The seven-hundred and fifty dollar per month fee would go toward rent and utilities.

I have to say I was not optimistic that my mother would be able to comply with this, would be able to handle this responsibility, but I really didn't have any other options at that point.

I signed the lease and my mother looked around the house, found her room, and set down her bags on one of the twin beds. All of her belongings fit in about a half-dozen Walmart bags. The stuff she kept consisted of coloring books, word puzzles, a couple of sweat shirts, a pair of pants, some slippers, and really whatever she was able to pilfer from the mental institution where she had been staying for the past month. It was nothing she would probably ever use, just more junk to add to her horde.

I told her that I'd take her to the store to get her first

week's supply of groceries, pick up her prescriptions, and maybe grab something to eat. I was surprised that as we drove around looking for the store that my mother was not mad at me for having her committed, for showing the psychiatrist the photographs I had taken of her house, for telling him how incapable I thought she was of living on her own. She actually seemed glad to see me again, to be with me, even if it was under these strange circumstances.

We went to Walmart and I let her pick out the items that she felt she needed, knowing from experience that she would likely never use these things. Often, she would take a loaf of bread, for example, unwrap the twist tie, then turn the tie over and over in her hands for a few minutes, run her fingers over the loaf of bread, then tie it back up, stare at it, pat it a few times, then walk away from it, never eating a crumb.

As my mother held my hand and walked closely to me as we went around the store, it was as though nothing had happened between us. It was not how you would expect someone who you just sent to a mental institution to act toward you. I realized then that her love for me was an unconditional one, which was probably a normal way for mothers to feel toward their children. I had never felt this before, and despite how odd the circumstances were I have to say that it felt nice knowing that I could do no wrong in my mother's eyes.

When we got back to the house, I helped my mother put away her groceries and organize her prescriptions into the new pill case I got for her. Then I handed her the first dosage, which the discharge papers from the hospital instructed me to give to her right away. My mother went into the bathroom to take her medicine, and I stayed in the kitchen putting away groceries. As I was doing this, a girl about my age came into the kitchen and introduced herself to me. She had a very distant look in her eyes and her speech was somewhat slurred. I knew that she was not drunk but that she was more likely on an anti-psychotic medication that was numbing her senses and flattening her affect like this. She stood very close to me as she talked, and I told her that my mother was going to be living there with her for a while, and that I was just here helping her to get settled in.

"Oh, cool," the girl said. "I can help you with those groceries. Just let me go put my bra on."

She looked down at her chest, then back up at me, still standing close, and if I hadn't spent a lot of time around people like her in the past few months, I would've been very uncomfortable standing next to her in this small kitchen, her looking at me in an almost-seductive way, something that said normal boundaries didn't exist there. And I have to be completely honest, there was something about that forward energy of her that I couldn't help but feel attracted to in some odd way. It's something that's hard to explain. It could be that it's comfortingly familiar to me to be around someone with little-to-no social boundaries, or what would generally be perceived as inappropriate behavior, since my mother's that way. I don't know. But after the girl walked off to her bedroom, looking back over her shoulder at me as she went up the stairs, I finished with the groceries and then went to check on my mother to see if she had taken her pill.

When I looked out of the back door, I saw my mother in the moonlit yard, a tiny white pill making its arc from her mouth to the grass next to the fence. I couldn't believe it.

"Susie, what the hell are you doing?"

"Nothing, *Da*vid," she said, placing a strong emphasis on the first syllable of my name like she does when she's angry or just being sarcastic or patronizing.

"I saw what you just did," I told her.

"So what. I told you I don't need that shit."

"Well you have to take it if you want to live here. It's the rules."

"I don't want to live here," she said. "I just want to go back home."

"To what? There's nothing there anymore. There's not even electricity."

"I don't believe that. Why would they cut off my electricity?"

"Why wouldn't they, Susie? You haven't even been there in months."

I could feel my anger already rising up. We started to argue. I told her that she had to stay there, that there was nothing left in Waveland, that she couldn't live with me again. She had no other choice, I told her.

"Okay," she said calmly. "Thank you, David."

I knew her too well by this point, though. She had already made up her mind and I was wasting my time talking to her.

I told her good-bye and drove home to my family. I'd been gone all day.

18.

My mother calls me anywhere from twenty to fifty times a day. Sometimes she leaves rambling messages, other times she just calls every other minute until I answer. I have to either turn my phone off or put it on MUTE when I'm at work or trying to accomplish anything around my house. When I finally do give in and answer, often beyond the point of frustration and exasperation, my mother will just want to talk about some mundane detail, like whether or not I still have that sheet of paper where she wrote out a list of things she wanted me to look for if I ever went back to her trailer in Waveland: a Ziploc bag full of quarters, a pair of Bobby's shoes, a pack of batteries.

So on this particular day, the day after I got her moved into the group home, I was not surprised that my phone was plagued with calls from Susie. Since my daughter was in a theater group, she had rehearsals and performances all that weekend, so my wife and I were juggling that with keeping my son entertained, and I simply did not have time to answer my phone. Maybe I should have.

Around ten o'clock that night, I was out at a Chinese buffet with my son while my wife and daughter were at one of their theater performances when an unknown number showed up on my phone. I recognized the 228 area code, though, and I decided to answer it. It was a police officer. He told me that he was from the Waveland Police Department and that he was at my mother's property. There was a cab driver there who was saying that my mother owed him one-hundred-and-fifty dollars, and that my mother was standing there in front of her dark trailer, her hand cut from when she tried to climb through one of the broken sliding glass doors.

"What?" I said.

"Your mother took a taxi from Baton Rouge, Louisiana, this afternoon. All the way out here to her place in Waveland. The driver says she owes him a hundred and fifty bucks. But she don't have it. Can you drive out here and pay this man, please?"

"I'm sorry," I told him. "It's ten o'clock at night, man. I have two little kids. That's over an hour's drive."

"Well, this guy said he'll lose his job if you don't pay him."

"Look, I'm sorry. But he shouldn't have driven her that far without getting some money from her up front. Why would he have done that anyway?"

"He's pretty pissed."

"Well, I'm sorry. I just can't help."

The officer hung up. I didn't know what to do. I had to keep reminding myself of all the things Susie has survived before, her "street smarts," how she's my mother, and that it's not the other way around. I was worried about her, but there was nothing I could do. I looked over at my son and helped him finish his plate.

The next morning I got another phone call. It was Jane, the social worker who helped me place Susie in the mental hospital after her suicide attempt. She talked to me as though she was an old friend by this point.

"Hey, David," she said. "How are you?"

"I'm fine. You?"

"Good. Look, David, we got your mom here again," she said.

"Where?"

"At the hospital. She had a heat stroke, we think. They have her on some fluids right now."

"What happened?"

"Well she was at her house, trying to stay in there in this heat, and she just couldn't take it. One of the neighbors saw her crawling down the street, and they called 911."

"Oh my God," I said.

"Can you come pick her up?"

"Today?"

"Well, as soon as possible. She can't really stay here, you know?"

"I know. Look, I'll try to come later on this afternoon."

"Okay," she said.

I spent the rest of that day driving all the way out to Waveland, picking my mother up from the hospital, then driving her back to Baton Rouge, where I dropped her off again at the group home. We didn't say a word to each other the entire time.

My mother didn't last long at that group home in Baton Rouge. Ms. Angela called me one morning and told me that

Susie was non-compliant, that she wouldn't bathe, wouldn't take her medication, and that she simply had to find somewhere else to live. Her and my mother had gotten into an argument over Susie's refusal to take a bath one day, and Ms. Angela had to physically push Susie into the bathroom and stand there watching her bathe. This wasn't good.

She gave me the litany of Susie's strange and frustrating behaviors—how she would stand for extended periods of time at the kitchen counter, rubbing her fingers across the packaging inside of a box of cereal, but that she would never eat it. How she would sit in the dark for hours, staring off into space. Ms. Angela asked if Susie had ever abused alcohol, I told her that she had, and her conclusion was that my mother was suffering from dementia. She said she had seen it before with people who had severe alcohol addictions. This may have been true, but truthfully, I think it was just her attempt to understand what the hell was wrong with my mother.

By this point I had spoken with so many doctors and received so many disparate diagnoses and frustrated responses—one psychiatrist who was about my age actually slammed his hands down on his desk in utter frustration at listening to my mother ramble incoherently about her childhood and the wrongs that had been inflicted upon her. I do understand, of course, that my mother was abused as a child and as a teenager, only to end up in an abusive marriage after losing me, but at some point, one simply has to take accountability for one's own behavior instead of constantly blaming everyone else. That particular young doctor even wrote on his daily log of my mother that she had the least amount of insight into her illness, which he deemed schizoaffective disorder, than anyone he had ever worked with.

Ms. Angela recommended another group home in Baton Rouge where she thought Susie might do a little better. It was called Indigent Partial Hospitalization. I had my doubts, but had no other options at this point. I called the director and spoke with her for a while, telling her about Susie's history and needs. The woman told me she would be delighted to meet my mother, and that she had a place for her if Susie was interested. Later that day, I drove out to Baton Rouge with my wife and kids, picked Susie up from Ms. Angela's house, and took her to the new group home.

The building was a nondescript, brick apartment complex, hidden behind an old strip mall and camouflaged by other similar buildings, the only thing distinguishing this place as being somehow different was the chain-linked fences surrounding the perimeter and the barred windows and doors. It looked like some sort of strange prison. The nearly-abandoned neighborhood was pocked with small churches, a laundromat, and basically empty streets with green Dumpsters on every other corner and a few people standing around on the sidewalks, their heads down.

We pulled into the empty parking lot (none of the occupants were allowed to drive) next to a white van with some sort of Baptist church logo on its large, sliding door. This, we would later learn, was the van in which the members of the group home would be transported to doctor's appointments, the grocery store, or to run any other errands they may have needed to do.

There was something very heavy about the atmosphere here, and my heart sank at the sight of it. Though the woman I had spoken with on the telephone was very sweet, I had a bad feeling about this place. It looked run-down, it smelled bad, and it was disconcerting that it was locked up like that. We had to ring a buzzer to get inside the large black gate at the entrance to the complex. My mother seemed unfazed. Surely, she had lived in worse places, I had to keep reminding myself, as she stoically followed behind us as we walked inside.

We spoke with the owner and she showed us around, went over the rules, and she spoke a little bit with my mother. I was heartened that the woman seemed to like Susie, a much different initial reaction to her than most people have. She laughed in a friendly way at Susie's myriad questions and patiently answered them all, even the ones Susie repeated a dozen times or more. She showed us the kitchen and the eating area, which looked like two single apartment units that had been converted into one large space. She told us that all the meals were communal, and that only snacks were allowed in the individual units, which contained one bedroom and one small bathroom shared by two people.

The kitchens had been mostly gutted out of them. A refrigerator and a small sink and some cabinets were all that remained. There was a gaping hole where the stove should have been. When I asked about this when being shown one of the empty apartments (it wasn't actually empty; it had been wrecked by the previous occupant and the owner was embarrassed when she opened the door to show us inside and discovered that no one had cleaned up the torn sheets, the scattered clothing and flipped mattresses, the garbage, the scrawling on the walls), she told me that they used to allow stoves in the units but that someone had once found a cat and cooked it alive in their oven. Hence the no pet/no stove policy.

I thought about what people would think of a son who would leave his mother in a place like this. I thought about the other option of letting her live in her trailer in Waveland. I asked my mother what she wanted to do, and of course, she wanted to come back and live with me at my house. I had my own family's safety to think about now and that was not an option for us anymore, I told her.

Susie told the owner of the group home that she would "think about it" when asked if she wanted to live there. I think she knew this was her last resort, but that she wanted to put it off as long as possible. Ms. Angela had told me earlier that Susie had until the end of the week to move out, and I think Susie wanted to make that time last as long as possible before settling in here. This was rock bottom, as they used to say to my dad at his AA meetings.

As we walked around the complex some more, there were people standing on the balcony, sitting in plastic chairs or on ice chests some of them. Almost all of them had that glazed-over look of people who are overly-medicated, a chemical straitjacket, they call it, and they would stare at you as you walked past, some of them would give a half-smile, but their eyes always remained averted from yours. It was as though a part of them understood, still, the shame of a place like this, of being thrown away from society, hidden back here behind an abandoned strip mall and camouflaged among similar-looking complexes; but those occupants could come and go as they pleased, even if it was just outside to a desolate, dark stretch of road leading nowhere.

On the morning when I was to take my mother from Ms. Angela's group home to the new complex where I had signed a six-month lease, I called Susie to tell her I was on my way. She never answered her phone once during the numerous calls I made. Still I made the drive out to Baton Rouge, pulled up to the house, and knocked on the door. No one answered. Her roommate was not there, Ms. Angela wasn't there, and for all I knew, neither was my mother. I knocked several more times, then turned the knob on the door to realize that it was not locked. I was immediately reminded of the time, only several months earlier, when I had discovered my mother's prostrate body after she took a bottle full of Librium to end her life with. I went inside.

The house was dark, quiet. I went up the narrow stairwell to the hallway where Susie's room was. Her roommate's door was open, her room blanketed with clothes and magazines, but she was not in there. I went to the end of the hallway and knocked on Susie's door. She didn't answer.

"Susie!" I called. "Are you in there?"

Still nothing.

I opened the door and inside the dark room Susie lay on her bed, completely dressed—even her shoes—sleeping. I could see her breathing and slowly she sat up and looked confusedly at me. None of her stuff was packed, even though she had known for days that she was moving. It was past noon.

"What the hell are you doing?" I said. "I've been calling you all morning. You have to leave this place today."

"What?" she said.

It was as though she were hearing this news for the first time.

The frustration from the past few months, the memories from all of my life, it seemed, started to well up inside of me again, and I knew I was about to lose it. I had to leave. I couldn't even look at her.

"Forget it. You're on your own," I said.

"Wait, David. I'll get ready. Just give me a few minutes." In her time-altered world, I knew, that could literally mean hours.

"No, I'm done. Find another ride out of here. I can't do this today."

Susie followed me down the narrow hallway, begging me to wait, saying she was sorry. I stopped to listen to her and she started moving toward the bathroom, then pulled off her jeans and started going to the bathroom right in front of me. I turned away, went down the stairs.

"Look, get your stuff packed. I'm leaving."

She called after me and I went back out to my car and sped out of the driveway. That was the last time I would ever see that place.

I drove around Baton Rouge for a while, crying and punching the steering wheel of my truck. I hadn't asked for any of this. I just couldn't deal with it anymore. Eventually, though, Ms. Angela transported my mother to her new home, eager, I'm sure, to get rid of her. Susie continued to call me numerous times each day, asking when I was going to take her back to her house in Waveland, when all of this was going to be over.

I visited her there a few times, took her out for ice cream once, which she said she hadn't eaten in thirty years. Bobby wouldn't let her, she said. And I wasn't surprised when I was dropping her back off at the group home one night and she told me that she would no longer be staying there. She said it just like that, too, very matter-of-factly, as though it were a decision she had pondered for a great while and had come to this final conclusion over. I asked her where she was going to go, and she said she wanted to go back to Waveland. It had been months since she had been "home" and she was ready to go back. I was tired, I was frustrated, I was worn down to the point of apathy. I told her, "Fine, Susie. If that's what you want, you got it. I'll pick you up this weekend and take you home."

"Really?"

"Yeah. I'm sick of hearing you talk about it."

"What about the electricity?"

"I'll get it turned back on."

"You will?"

"Yeah."

"What about Toby?" she said.

"You can have him back too."

She was elated. She hugged me good-bye and told me that she would be ready to go on Saturday.

I took the rest of the week and tied up the loose ends so that my mother could go back home. When I arrived in Baton

Rouge on Saturday, I helped her to fill up the back of my car with all of the things she had accumulated over the past six weeks. There were thick winter jackets that she had gotten from a Salvation Army, a pile of cell phones someone had given to her, clothes, sheets, books, papers, bag upon bag full of napkins and plastic utensils, whatever she could take from this place without it being noticed. She also had all of the virtually unused groceries I had gotten for her when she first came out here. We had to leave some things behind, as they would not even fit in my car. This was very difficult for her to do, and she actually asked me if I would come back out here later to gather the rest of her things. No way, I told her. No way.

When we got to Mississippi and pulled up to her lot, I could tell that something wasn't right. My mother noticed it too and jumped out of the passenger door while I was still driving toward her property. She ran up the steps and to the porch and then I could hear her screaming. Someone had pried off the piece of plywood I had covered her broken door with and had gone into her house, removing everything they could: they stole light sconces, the washer and dryer, the compressor and coils from the back of the refrigerator, the sheets from the bed. What they left behind was ransacked beyond comprehension: there was a half-foot of garbage and clothes and debris blanketing the entire floor.

My mother fell to her knees and cried. She couldn't move. She was paralyzed by shock. I was overwhelmed too, not because of what had happened here (it was mostly junk anyway, and the only thing of real value—the washer and dryer—had never even been used once, so I knew my mother wouldn't even miss that), but because now I had cancelled the lease to the group home and had nowhere left to take her. After I walked away from her and off into the woods where no one would hear me, I screamed as loud as I could, punching the side of a little scrub tree until I felt like I could breathe again. Then I went back and started trying to make sense of all of this mess.

I got things somewhat livable, which isn't hard to do in accordance to my mother's standards, repaired the door and put a new deadbolt on it, unpacked all of the things that Susie had put in the trunk of my car, and told her good-bye. I told her that I would be back each week to visit her and bring her groceries until we could work out a better arrangement. I was working with a new social worker from Adult Protective Services who was going to sign my mother up for Meals on Wheels. Later, my mother would refuse this service because she claimed she didn't know how to use a microwave in order to heat up the food—the *free* food that would be delivered to her front door, already warm, each and every day.

The last time I saw my mother I had just dropped her off at her house in Waveland after buying her a week's worth of groceries—bread, peanut butter, a dozen cans of Chef Boyardee, dog food, and milk—and like she usually did, she followed my car down the weeded driveway as I backed out, keeping her hand on the rolled-down window, still talking, trying to think of anything she could say to keep me from leaving. I had by now learned to just cut her off and make my way; otherwise, I would never leave. She told me to be careful, asked me when I was coming back to bring her more food, then verified my response by repeating it back to me—something she often did—she says it's so that the information will "stick in her head." Then she followed my car out to the gravel road.

I put it into DRIVE and started to inch away from her. She finally stopped and just stood there watching me leave. She was standing next to the weeded ditch, from which a rusted pole where a mailbox had once been jutted out from the hard ground next to a pile of dusty gravel that had never been spread over the driveway, behind that an old refrigerator with its coils pulled out, an old stove and a metal toolbox, all placed there by the thieves who had robbed her again and again and who would likely continue to do so, such was their desperation. This is where they put the things they intended to come back for later. My mother never bothered to move any of it. She never even bothered to call the police anymore when she saw the flickering of flashlights in her decrepit trailer, heard the muffled talking. She just let them take what they wanted. Someone had even taken all the STOP signs from the road leading up to my mother's house. Where she lived—had lived for over thirty years and had wanted to come back to so badly—was not a safe place.

There was a torn bed sheet—the one that had been on the bed which Elaine, her mother-in-law, had been in when we found her malnourished and near death—hanging from one of the leafless branches on a dead tree and whipping in the slight breeze as my mother squinted at my diminishing car, waving and then turning quickly and walking back to the chipped wooden steps leading up to her porch. I couldn't see her doing this, but I had seen it enough times before to envision her doing it now. I didn't know I would never see her again.

Such is the way of most significant events in our lives, my cutting myself off from my mother happened unexpectedly, though I probably knew in some deep part of me that it was inevitable. I hadn't planned to stop visiting her, to block her numbers from her collection of cell phones so that she could no longer contact me, to never write or speak to her again. It just sort of happened. I don't know how to offer any more satisfactory explanation than that. Now as time goes on it just seems more and more natural to be out of her life and to have her out of mine, though it doesn't feel good. But when does anything, any hard choice like this, feel good? In my experience it doesn't.

I still think about her, of course. I wonder how she's doing, if she's being taken care of properly by the people who are supposed to be taking care of her now. I wonder if she's forgiven me, or if she even thinks I've done anything wrong, that in her confused and disorganized and demented state if she even understands *why* I did what I felt I *had* to do. Not just for myself but for my wife and children. I've had to accept that my childhood didn't exist as it does for most people, that I'll never know the feeling of having a mother who loves me in a normal, healthy way, one I don't have to constantly have my guard up around to feel safe and secure, one who doesn't lie to me and take advantage of me.

I've been told that I've always acted older than my years, and I think I've had to do so out of necessity, and so that has aided me well throughout this ordeal. I have accepted that I will never have closure, never get the answers to the questions I have had my whole life, that I just have to have faith that something bigger than I am (and with more understanding of the workings of this universe than I have) will guide me and keep me on the path that I'm supposed to be on. Other than that, what else do I have?

One day my mother will die. Be it by her own hand or by the natural workings of time and the universe, this day will come. I like to think that I am prepared for it—that I have, in a sense, already accepted her death. In so many ways, it is as though she is already dead. I have tried to cut her from myself in the best and only way I know how to do. But still it hurts me. The pain of loss, the lack of closure, of no real ending to any of this. Just yesterday I was reading the newspaper and came across an article about a woman who had been found running naked through the Lowe's parking lot in Gulfport—about a mile from my mother's house. The report said that the woman was halfway clad in duct tape and that she had claimed she was raped in a nearby homeless camp (there are more than several tarp-covered camps in the woods near where my mother lives, and she's even come across some of these people trying to sleep among the debris in one of her trailers. This has been a mounting problem in the area ever since Hurricane Katrina).

My first thought upon reading this article was that the woman mentioned in it would turn out to be my mother. I had a sinking feeling in my stomach that it would be her. I just knew it. I waited to get a phone call from the police. In a way, this really wouldn't have surprised me after all my mother's done and been through: she's been known to hang out with what most people would consider the dregs of society—hell, some people would probably consider *her* to be that as well, though I don't.

Her husband once told me that my mother would run off with men for days or weeks at a time, exchanging sexual favors for drugs. I don't know if this is true or not, but from the things I've heard and seen, it wouldn't surprise me. My mother is a survivor: she has survived the emotional and physical abuse of her own mother, her husband, and countless others who prey on people like her. She survived Hurricane Katrina, hanging onto a pine tree for eight hours while the brown rushing water rose up to her neck, snakes and rats swimming past her as the wind threw her hair in knots, then later finding her way to a shelter where she would get the attention of a reporter from *National Geographic* who was down there doing a story on the hurricane's terrible, terrible aftermath. She would later have this reporter call our house in Folsom to tell us that Susie was okay and then ask if we would come get my mother from the shelter. She survived her husband's near death in 2000 and his death in 2012. She has survived losing her only child, possibly the worst tragedy of all for anyone. And she's still surviving to this day.

It turns out that the woman in the article was not my mother. It was some other poor woman, caught in the wrong place at the wrong time, a victim of the evil circumstances that unfortunately reside in the world, especially in the dark corners of homeless encampments in coastal Mississippi, a place that still wears its scars from Hurricane Katrina and even of Hurricane Camille before that. I'm relieved to know that my mother's at least okay for now. And I have to take this as a beginning, my own start of something new. I'll have to end this here, knowing that what more may come will be of my own making, and no one can take that away from me. No one.

Epilogue

To try to point at the genesis of my mother's mental illness would be futile: one can never know what causes these things. Is it a genetic roll of the dice, is it circumstantial, environmental, or a combination of all of these factors? I do know that my mother had part of her thyroid gland removed when she was in her early twenties, about a decade before I was born. After the surgery, against her doctor's orders, my mother left the hospital and went to a hair salon to have her hair cut and dyed—the large white bandage from the surgery was still taped to the side of her neck.

I also know that there is a sketchy history of mental illness in my family. My great-grandmother, for example, grew up in the Depression and had been treated with electroshock therapy at some point in her life. No one has said what for, though. She gave birth to my grandmother, moved across the country from Miami to California, remarried several times, leaving my *young grandmother home by herself for days at a stretch while she worked and went on dates with various men, one of whom allegedly climbed naked into the bed with my grandmother when she was a young girl.*

My grandmother also once told us about how someone in her family tied her to a tree sometimes so that she wouldn't stray outside of the yard while she was playing. It was on one of these occasions, she said, that a strange man pulled up next to her in his car and exposed himself, then pulled away quickly when she started to call out for help.

These things obviously had a profound effect on her mental well-being, which in turn caused her to become an alcoholic, an excessive worrier, and overall riddled with anxiety and depression. My grandmother was hospitalized as well, and I remember visiting her in the institution where she had been placed and playing horseshoes in the lawn with my brother and some of the other patients.

I knew also that my grandmother hated my mother. This may be hard to fathom—it is even for me, but my grandmother was young when she gave birth to my mother, had regretted the marriage she had jumped into, and did not want children. There are stories of her punching her pregnant stomach while my mother lay curled up in her womb, waiting to grow and be delivered into this world.

My grandmother told me that my mother would scream inconsolably for hours on end while she was an infant, that she knew even then that my mother was not normal. As my mother grew up, her behavior became even worse, and by the time she was a teenager, she was hearing voices. My grandmother and my mother fought incessantly, their altercations often turning physical. My grandmother once pushed my mother down a set of stairs, hit her in the arm with a rolling pin, and constantly slapped and hit her. Did these things cause my mother to become the woman she became? Or did they simply exacerbate an already-

existing chemical imbalance? It is impossible to know for sure.

My other great-grandmother, my grandfather's mother, was also not without her eccentricities. When my grandfather was a young boy, she left him, his older brother, and his younger sister with their father. She moved back to Honduras, where my grandfather was born, and remarried, having two more children. My grandfather and his siblings were placed in boarding schools —their father was a traveling salesman—and my grandfather's older brother eventually died while he was only twelve or thirteen years old.

When my grandfather's mother returned to the United States, she moved to New Orleans with her wealthy second husband who worked for a banana company, and she became notorious for shoplifting from all of the high-end department stores on Canal Street. Despite the money her husband made, she just couldn't help herself, stealing everything she could get her hands on. She would even steal the silverware and china from restaurants, once forgetting that she had placed a stack of plates and forks and knives in a napkin on her lap. When she stood up to leave the restaurant, the napkin and its contents spilled from her lap onto the floor, causing everyone to look over at her suspiciously. Her kleptomania got so bad at one point that, before she was officially banned from entering the department stores, her husband was actually paying a monthly stipend to a handful of their managers —things were done much differently back then—to cover the cost of all the things his wife stole. She later tried to poison him by pouring bleach into his drink one evening. The odor was so strong that he could smell it from where he sat in the living room, and everyone who was there visiting just sort of laughed it off, including him. These are all stories I heard growing up. It was as though my family was trying to justify my mother's behavior with them, and her subsequent decision for leaving me behind.

I have pictures of my great-grandmother the kleptomaniac—I called her GiGi—playing cards with me when I was little. She taught me how to gamble, I remember, and I can still see her in her gaudy hats with giant costume jewelry pinned to her jacket, the peacock feathers fanning out past her padded shoulders. She lived to be ninety-four, and I was in my twenties when she finally passed away. By then, she didn't know who any of us were.

When I was a boy, I remember getting birthday presents from GiGi, and I also remember dreading these gifts. Often they would arrive in a shirt box from some high-end department store like Macy's, Maison Blanche, or D. H. Holmes, and they always carried the smell of old mothballs or mold. But what was inside of them was anyone's guess.

She would fill these boxes with various toys and miscellany that had usually belonged to someone else before she gave them to me as presents; once I found an empty Noxzema jar filled with nickels (actually one of the best gifts she gave me), some cassette tapes I later learned she had stolen from her neighbors in the ritzy Esplanade Apartments where she lived across from City Park in New Orleans, water-stained books and papers, maybe a dirty rubber ball. But the worst and most humiliating gift she ever gave to me was a pair of girl's underwear. I was about ten years old and I remember opening the present and discovering this item, then recoiling from it as though there was a rattlesnake inside the box. I tried to hide the pink, lacy underwear under some of the other stuff so that my dad or my brother wouldn't see them, but it was no use. To this day, I can still feel the humiliation of that ten-year-old boy who is unsure of himself and who he is in the world, being totally shaken by what I perceived then as a heavily-symbolic gift. Now I know it was just her dementia or mental illness that caused her to give that to me.

People in my family would often remark that my mother had inherited the worst traits of each of her grandmothers. My grandmother would often say that's why she couldn't stand her oldest daughter so much: but it was more than that. When she was younger, my mother was beautiful and talented—she played the piano better than my grandmother had ever dreamed of playing, she was also an extraordinary painter and storyteller—she would entertain her younger siblings, and much later her nieces and nephews and sometimes even me, by telling stories of fantastical places and characters. In short, she was creative and had an artistic verve that was the envy of my grandmother, who wanted to be creative herself but just couldn't see past her own insecurities. So she took out her frustrations on her oldest daughter, my mother.

I've spent many years worrying that I would end up like my mother. I was vigilant in my early-to-mid-twenties for any signs of the disease which has all but ended her life. I would become anxious when family members would observe that a particular phrase I used or a physical expression I made was similar to hers. I knew I shared a lot of the same interests with my mother, despite my not being raised by her: my love of reading and ultimately of writing, my tendency toward creative endeavors such as keeping a sketch book, drawing, playing music in various bands as a teenager, always exploring the vistas of my imagination, creating a world for myself to which I could not only retreat, but from which I could return with information about what I had seen and experienced there. I would share these stories with those around me who might be interested, and sometimes even with those who were not. And while I am happy to have inherited these interests from her, I also worry that I may have inherited whatever else caused my mother to be who she was and still is.

I'm thirty-five years old now, and the problems I do have are not debilitating. While it's true that I suffer from obsessive-compulsive disorder and a mild case of anxiety and depression—all of which I take medication for—my disorders are not keeping me from being a father to my children, a husband, and a functioning member of society. And I don't "blame" my mother for these ailments that I have. In fact, I don't really blame her for anything. I've come to a place of acceptance and forgiveness in my life, and I am grateful for all that I have.

One final thing I've learned through all of these trials with my mother is that our mental health system in America is greatly flawed. People in need of help are not receiving it, are often homeless or left living as my mother does, alone and in squalor with no family able or willing to handle their disease. They are the victims of predators, robbers, thieves, and anyone looking to exploit them for their weaknesses.

There are laws prohibiting the long-term commitment of people like my mother, people for whom an institutionalized life may actually be beneficial. My mother seemed to function best when she was living in Gulf Oaks just after her suicide attempt and before her husband passed away. It was the structure, knowing what was expected of her, being given outlets for her frustrations and her creative energies, that kept her calm, I think. Yet these laws prohibiting long-term commitment are causing mental health professionals to scramble to find a place for the mentally ill. The result is that family members, like me, get "conned" into taking them in for a couple of days, just so the institution can have a document stating that the patient has a "plan" upon discharge. Though there is no real effort being made to follow-up on the patient, to make sure the patient receives the proper amount of after-care, that she continues to take her medication and to see her psychiatrist.

The group homes to which they are sometimes sent are not adequately supplied or staffed; these homes are being overwhelmed, their proprietors often taking advantage of a system that is so large and out of control that they are fraudulently collecting disability checks and misappropriating the funds for their own personal use, leaving the tenants in squalor with little food, and just barely providing them with the basic necessities.

Some would say that it is unfair to "lock people up" who have not committed a crime. But after my experience with my mother, I think that people like her need to be taken care of by professionals, kept in a structured environment with rules and expectations.

People like my mother could actually thrive in a place like this. Right now, though she is "free," she is barely surviving. I think she is even in danger.

People like my mother are the forgotten, the unwanted; they are living in homeless camps, "tent cities" in the woods behind strip malls and big box stores. They are standing on the sides of the intersections with cardboard signs, begging for change. They are mothers, fathers, sons, daughters, veterans, artists. They become drug addicts, alcoholics, hoarders, utilizing anything they can to quell their demons.

I hope that one day something can be done to better help people like my mother. I hope that all of the mentally ill, the downtrodden, the addicted, the hopeless, the forlorn, all of them can get the care that they need, that they deserve. And I hope that one day perhaps I can help make that happen. Maybe this is a start.

DAVID ARMAND was born and raised in Louisiana. He has worked as a drywall hanger, a draftsman, and as a press operator in a flag printing factory. He now teaches at Southeastern Louisiana University, where he also serves as associate editor for Louisiana Literature Press. In 2010, he won the George Garrett Fiction Prize for his first novel, *The Pugilist's Wife*, which was published by Texas Review Press. His second novel, *Harlow*, was published by Texas Review Press in 2013. David's third novel, *The Gorge*, was published by Southeast Missouri State University Press in 2015. A chapbook, *The Deep Woods*, was also published in 2015 by Blue Horse Press. David lives with his wife and two children and is working on his sixth book, *The Lord's Acre*.